BRITISH GOVERNMENT

AND ITS DISCONTENTS

BRITISH GOVERNMENT AND ITS DISCONTENTS

GEOFFREY SMITH

&

NELSON W. POLSBY

Basic Books, Inc., Publishers   *New York*

Library of Congress Cataloging in Publication Data

Smith, Geoffrey, 1930–
    British government and its discontents.

    Includes bibliographical references and index.
    1. Great Britain—Politics and government—1945–
2. Great Britain—Economic policy—1945–   3. Great
Britain—Foreign relations—1945–   4. Great Britain—
Social policy. I. Polsby, Nelson W., joint author.
II. Title.
JN234 1980.S64   320.941   79–56372
ISBN: 0–465–00765–1

To the joys of collaboration

with

Elizabeth Smith

and

Linda O. Polsby

The British do not say "You're welcome" and they seldom shake hands. What they do best is empty trash . . . deliver mail and milk at dawn, run schools, provide dental and medical care and eyeglasses for a pittance, broadcast intelligent radio programs, plant pretty gardens, produce articulate debate, maintain the character of villages and parks, brew real beer, finance a spectacularly good library service, stand politely in line, avoid talking to strangers and make amateurism and uncompetitiveness the goals of nearly every endeavor. There is no money in this.

—Paul Theroux
The New York Times
Book Review

CONTENTS

Contents

PART III
INSTEAD OF A CONCLUSION

PREFACE

This book originated the way collaborations ought to begin—in conversation. We found ourselves engaged in fairly intense discussions about British politics: why not record them and see whether the pleasure and instruction we were shamelessly deriving from hearing our own voices could be spread among a larger population? At the start of our conversations, in the spring and summer of 1978, the direst and most apocalyptic visions of British prospects in the world were no longer dominating the bookstalls or the serious newspapers, but nothing more optimistic had come along to take their place. British politics bumbled along in a lull before an election. Figures on inflation were for the moment on the way down. British balances of payments had been in the black for one or two consecutive months. There were clouds on the horizon, of course; in Great Britain there always are, when they are not closer than the horizon. But they were no bigger than the hands of a few score men and, perhaps, one woman.

What better time than in an unaccustomed pause between crises to begin to survey the interrelations, complex enough even in normal circumstances, between British government and the social and political problems with which the government must somehow cope? For the better part of a year, one of us had been attempting to educate himself in the intricacies of the British political scene. The other fell into the habit of periodically sharing his ideas on an informal basis. Some of these ideas we thought might be obvious to insiders but at the same time news to the vast majority of readers, in Britain and elsewhere. And thus we had the rationale for this survey of British government, its problems and prospects, written for people who may understand something of politics but do not necessarily know the details of British politics.

The focus of this book on British government and its discontents reflects the concerns of a British journalist who traffics in ideas and information about the problems of his time and place, and of an American political scientist who seeks to understand long-term forces that account for problems and point toward, and away from, solutions. Neither of us thinks Britain's discontents are exclusively cultural, or psychological, or political, or economic. We focus on political remedies because politics is the realm of proximate causes, of manipulable factors—the realm, in short, of the possible. Neither of us thinks that there is reason to despair of contemporary Britain, and both of us believe that half-measures are not only better than none but sometimes better than whole measures. Many benefits and costs attend life in a middle-aged, middle-sized, formerly prosperous, presently semi-collectivized, freedom-loving, intensely tribal, modern society with tired blood, cultivated civil servants, weak industries, strong unions, and a flourishing high culture. These and other disparate elements fit together in a unique pattern in Britain; nevertheless, we are interested in how British experience compares with other democratic nations. We are concerned not only with warnings and cautionary tales, but also with hidden resources and unexpected strengths.

This book began as a tutorial in the elements of contemporary

British politics. The agenda was mostly structured by the flow of American questions. Most of the answers, naturally, come from the British half of the collaboration. The final product, however, is the result of much exchange back and forth over an extended period, and we take joint responsibility for the present form in which our dialogue has been cast.

ACKNOWLEDGMENTS

The obligations we have incurred in the course of learning what we needed to know to write this book are too many and too varied to record. And so we restrict our expressions of gratitude to those individuals and organizations who have helped us most directly. First and foremost, our thanks to Elizabeth Smith, who provided the hospitality and the indispensable skill at operating a tape recorder that made possible the original text from which our book evolved.

The Institute of International Studies, the Committee on Research, the Institute of Governmental Studies, and the National Policy Studies Program—all of the University of California, Berkeley—provided ways and means for us to spend time together, and clerical help in finishing the manuscript. We also thank Linda O. Polsby, Helen Petit, and Philip Wilson in Berkeley for extraordinarily helpful and timely assistance.

The John Simon Guggenheim Foundation and the University of California provided one of us with the sabbatical time that is the prerequisite of extensive and concentrated work.

Acknowledgments

Several friends and colleagues read drafts of various chapters and gave us advice or encouragement, and sometimes both. We thank William M. Drower, Leslie Lipson, Aaron Wildavsky, Linda O. Polsby, Elizabeth Smith, and George W. Jones for their kindness and their efforts in our behalf. We absolve them from responsibility for what we have written, however, in the secure knowledge that in at least some respects they do not fully agree with us.

Midge Decter and Phoebe Hoss of Basic Books were a pleasure to deal with. Our readers have good reason to be as grateful to them as we are.

GEOFFREY SMITH
NELSON W. POLSBY

London
Berkeley
June 1980

xvi

PART I

BRITAIN'S POLITICAL AGENDA:

ECONOMIC PRODUCTIVITY,

SOCIAL SOLIDARITY,

INTERNATIONAL INFLUENCE

It is now commonplace to view Great Britain as a nation beset by problems. No doubt the foremost among these is a laggard economy. Some commentators do not stop there, however, and claim to observe a general slackening of spirit, a shrinkage of expectations and ambitions, a more comprehensive malaise in British society.

The evident interpenetration of economic, social, psychological, and political conditions poses difficulties for analysis. Our own approach is to begin by outlining three central problems that, more than any other, seem to us to dominate contemporary British life and to set the agenda for British politics in the foreseeable future. These are the problems of economic productivity, of social solidarity, and of international influence.

1

CHAPTER 1

Do You Sincerely Want
To Be Rich?

It has become fashionable over the last twenty years to regard Britain not just as a country with problems but as a problem country. Studies are available on what is wrong with nearly every aspect of British life—with British industry, schools, housing, hospitals, public services of all sorts. The list has been long. More recently the whole of British society itself has come to be seen as the problem. It is the collapse of Britain that has been postulated, and not least often by friendly critics from overseas.

Inevitably there is an element of fanciful exaggeration when conversation is captured by images and metaphorical language. No matter how great the difficulties of the inhabitants, the British Isles are not really going to subside ignominiously into the Atlantic Ocean. There is in actuality no drain somewhere in the North Sea into which Britain is likely to disappear. The evidence does not support the more lurid theories of disintegration. It does suggest progressive decline, however; and only in a country suffering from a severe loss of confidence would it be possible, as in Britain, to found a growth industry on the analysis of failure.

What is the reason for this pervasive sense of failure? At one level Britain's record since the Second World War may be seen as a success story. Over these past thirty-five years Britain has become a more prosperous country. The British people have more money in their pockets, enjoy better housing, have more modern appliances in their homes, run more cars, work a shorter day, week, and year, take more holidays at home and abroad, and have improved health care—most of it free at the point of delivery. Pensions are higher, and sickness and unemployment insurance covered by the state are virtually comprehensive for the working population. So material security in and out of work is much enhanced for most individuals in Britain compared with their condition in 1945—and even more so compared with the years before the war.[1]

British living standards have, in short, risen enormously; but throughout this period a rising standard of living has been the common experience of all nations in the Western world. It is when one compares the British performance with that of other Western countries that a gloomy picture emerges. The growth in real terms of the national product was less in the United Kingdom in the decade from 1965–66 to 1975–76 than in OECD (Organization for Economic Cooperation and Development) countries as a group or in any single one of the other leading OECD members—the United States, Japan, Germany, France, Canada, or Italy. In the years since then, only in 1978 did the United Kingdom just manage to lift itself out of last place when it had a growth rate a little above Italy's and equal to that of France and Germany.[2]

Output per man-hour in manufacturing rose by less in the United Kingdom between 1970 and 1978 than in any of these other nations, while hourly earnings in manufacturing rose by more than in any of them—except Japan, where the increase had been justified by the highest rise in output, and Italy, which has been challenging Britain closely for the worst economic record in Western Europe. So it can occasion little surprise to observe that United Kingdom consumer prices rose more during this period than those of any of these other countries.[3]

4

Do You Sincerely Want To Be Rich?

Strangely enough, the British strike record, which attracts so much unfavorable notice at home and overseas, is no worse than in many other countries. In terms of working days lost, it is better than that of the United States, though this record does not make nonsense of all the talk about the pernicious effect of the unions on the British economy. Rather, the damage that the unions inflict is felt not so much through the strikes that actually take place as through threats of strikes. These threats have a paralyzing effect upon management and have persuaded many British managers to give up to the unions the prerogatives—and the responsibilities—of the managerial role. In Britain a higher proportion of the work force belongs to a union than in most of Britain's industrial rivals—certainly more than in the United States; and the number of unions having weak central control is growing.[4] Thus, the unions have more power, and they are harder to negotiate with because they are so often in conflict internally and with each other.[5]

Yet it might plausibly be maintained that none of these facts should have a depressing effect upon national morale so long as real living standards are rising. Economic statistics are not such popular bedside reading that they send the nation into an anguished and restless sleep each night; and the activities of the unions may be thought to benefit their numerous members, even if these activities are a cause of distress to those differently situated, or to those who have, or choose to take, a broader view of the national interest. So long as the British are doing well, who should worry that the Americans, the French, and the Germans are doing better?

The answer is that the British worry partly because so many of them travel abroad and can see for themselves the higher living standards in other European countries which they were accustomed to regard as less economically advanced, partly because conditions in other countries are visible on television even to those who never travel overseas, and partly because they are told to worry. A profusion of analyses and forecasts has drawn attention to Britain's less favorable circumstances—and the British are no less capable of envy than other people—and to the unlikely prospect of even an absolute improvement in British living conditions, as British industry finds it progressively harder to compete at home —never mind competing abroad.

Lord Rothschild, when he was head of the Central Policy Review Staff, the government's own think tank, warned in 1973 that on current trends Britain would become one of Europe's poorest countries by 1985. The Hudson Institute in the early 1970s drew a picture of Britain sliding ignominiously toward the 1980s.[6] And Sir Nicholas Henderson, who subsequently became the United Kingdom's ambassador in Washington, presented an analysis of almost unrelieved gloom in what he thought was his valedictory dispatch as a member of the British Foreign Service when he retired as ambassador to France in March 1979:

> Income per head in Britain is now, for the first time for over 300 years, below that in France. We are scarcely in the same economic league as the Germans or French. We talk of ourselves without shame as being one of the less prosperous countries of Europe. The prognosis for the forseeable future is discouraging. If present trends continue we shall be overtaken in GDP per head by Italy and Spain well before the end of the century.[7]

These are among the jeremiads that have attracted the most public notice in recent years, but they are by no means the only examples. Some have been more closely reasoned than others, but their cumulative effect has been to impress upon the British an awareness of Britain's relative failure rather than to celebrate its absolute improvement in living standards.

So the British malaise is both a psychological condition and, as is evident in the economic statistics, more than a psychological condition. It does not follow, therefore, that Britain's difficulties should be seen simply in economic terms. On the contrary, we believe that economic failings have been the product of political conditions, with "political" interpreted in the broadest sense to incorporate both attitudes and institutions.

First, there is the question of individual attitudes in Britain. A few years ago there was a book with the title "Do You Sincerely Want to Be Rich?" So far as the majority of British people are concerned, they have not sincerely wanted to be rich. They have evidently preferred to rank higher the comforts of a unique way of life. Throughout the postwar years, in comparison not only with other countries but with British life in previous generations, Britain has been a country in which it has been exceedingly comfortable to live. In the face of great social change—the loss of empire, the liquidation of investments abroad, the establishment of a welfare state—a sense of fundamental decency has, on the whole, been preserved in British society. Strong norms of family life have been sustained in Britain, as well as the sense of local social identity. Geographic mobility, especially in the working class, is far less than in the United States, where it has contributed significantly both to economic growth and to social instability. Frequently the British prefer to stay close to their family and friends—and their low-rent council houses—rather than to move away in search of promotion, or even of a job. But it may well have been necessary to sacrifice some of these social advantages if economic success was to be achieved.

That the British have not been prepared to pay this price has been applauded by cultivated foreigners of good will. Bernard Nossiter, the former London correspondent of the *Washington Post,* argues in his book *Britain: A Future That Works,* that the deliberate preference for leisure is the mark of a civilized and mature people.[8] Thus, Britons should be praised, not blamed, for this attitude. If, however, this tribute to the judgment of the British people is to be fully justified, they would have to be ready with equal deliberation to meet the costs of their leisure. "Take what you want—and pay for it, says God." So run the words of the proverb. But the British people have not been prepared to pay for their leisure, at least not on a pay-as-you-go basis. They are to be compared rather to the man who chooses to lie late in bed in the morning but does not choose to be late for work.

The lack of zest on both the labor and the management sides of industry, and the reluctance to change, almost guarantee an inferior economic performance. Yet massive wage claims keep flowing in with no apparent absence of zeal. Britain presents the paradox of an unambitious society that is not content with the fruits of its relaxation.

There has also been a loss of national confidence which is to be explained not solely by the demoralizing effect of standing low in the economic league, but by the decline in Britain's relative international status. Britain emerged from the Second World War with a standing as one of the great powers in the world. This perception of Britain's position at that time was exaggerated. Britain's economic and material weakness as the result of wartime expenditures had progressed so far that it was no longer realistic, even then, to consider it as a principal international power.

Since then the decay in Britain's status has been rapid. The Empire has disappeared; the Commonwealth is no substitute. Nor has membership in the European Community provided Britain with an alternative power base in the sense of enabling it to carry the same weight in the world. In military, economic, or diplomatic terms Britain does not possess the authority or the influence that it once did.

In itself the loss of power may not seem to matter much. The number of people who were able to draw direct satisfaction from Britain's imperial role was limited. Not many could enjoy the pomp of being a viceroy of India. Few in any age can experience the sense of power that comes to the leading figures in international diplomacy. It is therefore easy to dismiss the consequences of Britain's decline in international standing as simply the nostalgia of a ruling elite for a world in which others were required to make sacrifices for the greater glory of the United Kingdom.

That estimation ignores, however, the indirect satisfactions that come to the citizens of a country that has weight in the world's affairs. All of us are deeply influenced by the fortunes of the wider groups to which we belong, from the family outward—and the nation-state is the political grouping that remains the primary focus of loyalty for most people in the Western world. We are nearly all—however dimly—conscious of the figure that our country cuts on the international scene. There is a pride in belonging to a major nation which compels the respect of others; and—more to the point—there is a withdrawal of pride in belonging to a country that has ceased to enjoy that status. The relationship between national pride and performance is subtle and not simple; but the loss of pride can permeate all corners of a nation's life, creating a society at odds with itself.

That British society is at odds with itself is evident from current domestic anxiety over structures and processes of government. Traditionally British political stability has been the wonder of other nations. Its institutions have been secure. Its parliamentary democracy has been exported with more enthusiasm—and more takers—than many of its other products. But now there is dissatisfaction with the operation of Parliament, with the safeguards for individual freedom provided by the constitution, with the relationship between the elected government and both sides of industry, particularly the trade unions, with the role of the political parties and the excessive power of the Civil Service. One part of the United Kingdom, Northern Ireland, has been in ferment for over a decade, and its future is in question; and the constitutional relationships between the smaller nations, Scotland and Wales, and the rest of the United Kingdom have been the cause of much concern. No longer is there the automatic belief that Britain is a successful, well-run country which can look with superiority, tempered by compassion, on the way in which others do things in less fortunate lands.

This constitutional discontent may be, at one level, a symptom of a wider malaise. It is when things are going badly that people are most likely to be concerned about processes and about reforming them. If the water gushes forth from a leaky pipe that has supposedly been mended by a plumber who has been hired on the recommendation of a friend, we are likely to reflect in our dampness whether we might not have done better some other way.

Whether the plumber is ordinarily good or the pipe bad, or the friend sound in his judgment, we are likely to feel that if only the process of selection is better next time, we shall not suffer again. It is because British society has not been delivering the goods that the processes of government have been brought so much in question.

Constitutional discontent is more than just a symptom. It relates directly to some of the most important substantive problems facing Britain. This relationship is most obvious in the case of Northern Ireland. A few years ago it looked as if the future of Scotland also might be one of those delicate issues that would disturb the United Kingdom for years to come. The rise and decline both of Scottish nationalism and of the demand for devolution—the creation of subordinate assemblies for Scotland and Wales within the United Kingdom—are examples of the extent to which constitutional discontent has provided the government of the United Kingdom with pressing practical challenges. When social solidarity and political cohesion is threatened in a country like Britain, whose tradition has been essentially that of unitary rule, the difficulty is much greater than is readily appreciated by those with a political heritage that better accommodates fragmentation. The stability of the United Kingdom has depended so much upon the authority of the central government that, when the center is weakened, cracks are likely to appear in different parts of the structure.

Another reason that the structures and processes of government now loom so large in British consciousness is that the decisions of government, both central and local, have become more consequential and more pervasive in people's lives. This situation is most conspicuous in the economic sphere.[9] The White Paper on Employment Policy published in 1944 by Winston Churchill's wartime coalition government is generally regarded as marking a turning point in adding to the responsibilities of government the maintenance of a high and stable level of employment after the war.[10] This increase in the scope of government may not seem, in the changed atmosphere of today, to be at all remarkable. It may appear to have

been no more than an acknowledgment of the political requirements that the electorate would be bound to place upon any government after the grim experience of the depression between the
wars, as is suggested by its exact analogue in the American Full
Employment Act of 1946.[11] It meant in any event that no government could henceforth shrug off national economic distress as the
work of an unkind providence and an inconvenient trade cycle. In
taking responsibility for employment, government took on ultimate responsibility for the economy as a whole. No longer could
government's task be interpreted as simply securing the basic conditions for a civilized and ordered community while individual
citizens and private firms got on with the business of creating
wealth. If prosperity was not achieved, if prices rose, then the
government of the day would be held to blame.[12]

The accumulation of responsibility in governmental hands has
meant that the test of governmental efficacy has become all the
more difficult, and that many people throughout the country stand
to lose directly and personally if government fails to meet the test.
Any incompetence, any harshness, any unfairness in government
bears down upon individuals as never before—so that the proper
operation of the processes of government are no longer a matter of
purely academic concern.

This trend has, of course, been evident in most other highly
industrialized democratic countries in the postwar world. But
there are some observers who maintain that the peculiar circumstances of British life, with its particular juxtaposition of political
and economic forces, make this an exceptionally difficult and even
dangerous set of obligations in the United Kingdom. One of the
most influential criticisms of British society in recent years was
made by Peter Jay while he was economic editor of *The Times* and
before he became Britain's ambassador in Washington. He put
forward the proposition that in modern democratic countries there
are four objectives that are not compatible: full employment, stable
prices, free collective bargaining, and political democracy. A democratic electorate will require its government to guarantee full

11

employment, and the trade unions will insist upon free collective bargaining, apart from the relatively brief periods when governments are able to enforce pay restraint. But if collective bargaining is free, the unions will secure wage increases that force prices up to the point where the demand for goods will fall, and full employment will be jeopardized unless the government injects more money into the economy in order to maintain effective demand. This development will in turn cause a further surge of inflation and another round of the vicious circle. These dangers are particularly great in Britain where the trade unions are much stronger than in many countries, including the United States. Governments cannot in such circumstances meet expectations for full employment and political freedom, so that a point will ultimately be reached where democracy itself is brought in question.[13]

There is no need to agree wholly with Mr. Jay's analysis to appreciate its significance. Indeed, he himself, perhaps encouraged by his official responsibilities, was later to modify it. Democratic electorates have in fact shown that they can take a fair amount of economic disappointment, and nowhere more than in Britain.[14] Trade union leaders do respond, even if imperfectly, to what they perceive the economic circumstances to be. They can take fright on occasion like anybody else. What is significant to us in Mr. Jay's diagnosis is that he sees Britain's economic problem in essentially political terms. How are the conflicting interests in British society to be reconciled? How is the power of the trade unions to be contained without destroying the democratic basis of the political system?

These are fundamentally problems of political authority. In theory, such problems are the ones that Britain should find easiest to solve—a country with a long and proud history, united for centuries, possessing a tradition of strong central government. Yet for some years now a paradox of authority has lain at the heart of Britain's difficulties. In constitutional terms British governments are indeed strong. We shall refer later to Lord Hailsham's discussion of the problem of an elective dictatorship, where a minority of the British people can elect a government that exercises the full powers of the constitution without any effective checks and balances until the voters next get the chance to pronounce their verdict. Between elections, as a matter of constitutional entitlement, the government of the day has immense power.

Yet nobody observing the British scene in recent years could suppose that United Kingdom governments are all-powerful in practical terms. Edward Heath's Conservative government found its authority so challenged by the trade unions that in February 1974 he called an election to settle the question, "Who rules Britain?" He lost that election. Indeed, the power of the unions has presented the most formidable checks on the capacity of successive administrations to govern Britain.[15] In 1969, Harold Wilson's Labour government decided that the activities of trade unions needed to be brought more within the scope of the law. It was not that British unions were indulging in the corrupt and illegal practices that disfigure the record of some American unions. Rather, in the course of this century British unions have been given certain immunities at law which enable them to conduct their affairs largely as they please and to employ a broad range of tactics now frequently regarded as illegitimate in furtherance of a trade dispute.

The Wilson government's proposals were set out in an official white paper, *In Place of Strife,* drawn up by Barbara Castle, then Secretary of State for Employment.[16] But such was the force of opposition within the labor movement that Mr. Wilson and Mrs. Castle had to abandon their intention to legislate on the principal recommendations of the white paper, and had to content themselves with assurances of good behavior from the trade unions. The resistance to *In Place of Strife* came from the trade unions themselves, from their friends in and out of Parliament, and from those in the Cabinet who valued their trade union connections—most notably the Home Secretary, James Callaghan. Ultimately Mr. Wilson and Mrs. Castle were unable to win the support of their own Cabinet to push the legislation through Parliament. The practical authority of the government had melted away, despite its

13

comfortable parliamentary majority, when challenged by such an interest group.

The Heath government, which succeeded the Wilson administration of 1969, was a little more successful on this issue, managing to get its Industrial Relations Act of 1971 on the statute book. But it was not able to make the act effective; and the resentment that the enactment of this law provoked within the trade union movement helped to strengthen opposition to the government when the latter came into conflict with the miners over pay in 1973 and 1974.[17] Thus, two successive governments of differing political complexion proved unable to use their supposedly unlimited constitutional authority to bring the power of the unions within new legal limits.

No subsequent government has attempted to make changes of great magnitude in industrial relations law—unless one regards the repeal of the 1971 act by the succeeding Labour government and the modest reforms of the Thatcher government in this light—so the strength of the unions remains central to Britain's economic problems. The unions are able to enforce practices that curtail productivity and consequently restrict the incentive to invest. And their influence inhibits economic policy in other ways.

In the summer of 1961, Harold Macmillan found his government confronted by what he described as a major problem of a novel character. "Our difficulties," he said, "were primarily due to the simple fact that rising personal demand was not being met by rising productivity." His answer was to institute what he termed a "pay pause."

> The pay pause of 1961–62 was the first—no doubt amateurish—attempt to move towards what has afterwards become known as an "incomes policy." Since the concept was novel, and the leaders of the trade unions in Britain are conspicuous for their conservatism, the pay pause not unnaturally resulted in serious political difficulties and pressures as well as the prospect of widespread conflict involving bitter opposition to the Government of the day.[18]

In the intervening years the concept of an incomes policy has become far from novel in Britain, but the political difficulties have remained as serious. A familiar pattern has developed. An incomes policy is introduced in circumstances of emergency and alarm as the country faces a wage explosion. The first round, consisting of a freeze—or more likely a low ceiling on wage increases for everyone—works reasonably well. The second round, allowing for some exceptions—possibly incorporating productivity agreements—is nearly as successful. But by the third or fourth annual round the dam bursts. The restrictions of such a policy are no longer acceptable in practice, even when a large majority of the country still approves of the principle. This, roughly, was the history of the incomes policy of the Wilson and Callaghan governments from 1975 to 1979.

In part incomes policies of this kind do not work for long because no British incomes policy has yet provided for the delicate adjustments in pay between one group and another which soon become necessary in any economy that is at all responsive to changing conditions. It may be that no incomes policy can be operated indefinitely—or at least not in Britain where there is such weak central control within the trade union movement. But alternatives to incomes policy also require a measure of political consent that is not assured in Britain today.

The logic of relying upon monetary restrictions to control inflation—the policy with which Mrs. Thatcher's Conservative government took office in May 1979—is that the government should ensure that the money is not available to finance inflationary wage settlements. If the availability of money is controlled, and the trade unions still insist upon negotiating raises for their members above the level that a given industry can support, marginal companies will go out of business and workers will lose their jobs. If the unions fear this eventuality enough to exercise restraint—which they will do if the government makes credible its threat of monetary discipline—then inflation can be held in check. Otherwise, to be effective, this method of inflation control will lead to increases, possibly massive increases, in unemployment. Such a policy presents the problem of maintaining political consent, not merely backing for the government but perhaps even the consent necessary to maintain public order.

Unless political consent is forthcoming, no anti-inflation policy will work. The intense debate along economic lines that has taken place between the two main schools of thought in Britain in recent years—advocating either an incomes policy or monetary restraint—has not taken this fact fully into account. Arguments over economic strategy are secondary, in our view, to the problem of creating political conditions for any economic policy to be successful. How can these conditions be secured?

There is no magical answer to such a question. The mood of a nation cannot be manipulated by simple procedural reforms. Allowance must be made for much that is intangible. One possible approach is for the government to seek not to impose its will upon the principal interest groups of the nation but to involve them in a collective responsibility for running the country's affairs. This line of thinking was perhaps most clearly expressed by Mr. Heath as Prime Minister when, at the Conservative Party Conference in October 1972, he called upon employers, unions, and government to work out together how to create and share the nation's wealth for the benefit of all the people. "It is an offer to employers and unions to share fully with the Government the benefits and obligations involved in running the national economy." He went on to spell out the implications of this offer: "We know that we can look ahead year by year to consider the means of creating further expansion, and to agree on the priorities to which the nation wishes to devote its increasing wealth."[19] It is the second half of that sentence that is significant. The unions and the employers were being offered a share in deciding not merely how the economy should be run but also how the national income should be distributed. This offer would presumably have included consultation on both the level and the apportionment of taxation, and the allocation of public expenditure. The whole range of social and other policies that

16

previously had been the prerogative exclusively of government to determine, even if it discussed its decisions with others, would under such an arrangement have been subject to collective agreement. This power would have been granted in return for the acceptance of a voluntary incomes policy.

The idea proved stillborn on this occasion: Mr. Heath was unable to win the agreement of his prospective partners. When the attempt to forge the Tripartite Agreement, as it became known, collapsed in November 1972, Mr. Heath immediately instituted a statutory freeze on pay and prices.

The Labour government which succeeded Heath's administration in 1974 rejected the idea of a compulsory incomes policy, but it took further the concept of a national bargain between the government and the unions. That reasoning underlay the Social Contract that formed the basis of the incomes policies of the Wilson-Callaghan governments. The first two phases of the policy, from the summer of 1975 to 1977, had the full support of the Trades Union Congress (TUC). Indeed, the form of the first phase—a ceiling of six pounds a week on wage rises for everyone earning up to eighty-five hundred pounds a year, and no increase for anyone above that level—had actually been devised by Jack Jones, then general secretary of the largest British union, the Transport and General Workers Union. The third phase had the acquiescence of the unions, though not their open approval; and the fourth phase collapsed—a failure that contributed to the fall of the Callaghan government.

While it lasted, therefore, the incomes policy of the Labour years had either the active or the tacit backing of the trade unions. In return the unions were given considerable influence over government policy over a wide spectrum. The Industrial Relations Act of 1971, which they hated, was replaced by the Trade Union and Labour Relations Act, which restored and even extended their prerogatives. Retirement pensions were raised higher than they would otherwise have been in response to Mr. Jones's pressure. And nobody who observed the operations of the British government at that time would have questioned the sensitivity of ministers to the wishes of trade union leaders on any aspect of government which touched their interests.

The advantage of such a strategy is that it rides with the tide of power in society. The strength of the interest groups becomes an ally of government, rather than a challenge to authority. Instead of fighting a battle that it may not be able to win, the government seeks to cooperate with interests that may be too powerful to be coerced and are certainly too large to be ignored. British affairs, it is clear, cannot be managed effectively for any length of time in defiance of the united opposition of either side of industry.

But there are two reasons that it is not, over the long run, possible to rely too much upon such a strategy. The first is that there could be no assurance under British conditions that any of the principal interest groups could deliver its side of the bargain. Nobody really speaks for the whole of British industry. The Confederation of British Industries (CBI) comes nearest to doing so, but it is not altogether clear how far it speaks for companies and how far for managers as a class. On the union side, the relative weakness of the TUC at the center has already been noted. The leaders of individual unions have also experienced increasing difficulty in recent years in controlling their own members, when the members felt that their personal interests were being subordinated to national or union policy. Otherwise the Callaghan incomes policy would have received trade union backing for longer than it did. It was because they were conscious of pressure from their rank-and-file that most of the union leaders rejected the fourth phase of his policy, and the industrial disruption that broke out in the early months of 1979 principally reflected restiveness on the shop floors.

The second reason for not relying too much upon the collaboration of interest groups is that such groups cannot speak for the interests of all members of the public—or, indeed, for all the interests of even their own members. Trade unionists are consumers as well as producers. So there are reasons of principle as well as practicality for seeking other means of securing the necessary degree of political consent for the affairs of a free society to be conducted successfully.

This is a problem that causes anxiety in other democratic countries, including the United States, and is likely to do so increasingly. In more educated societies, where neither the word of authority nor the advice of the expert are unhesitatingly accepted, the wisdom of those who are elected to office is no longer taken for granted. Among larger proportions of the increasingly well educated populace, there is a visible demand for direct influence upon policies. So it is necessary to consider whether the traditional instruments for governing large democratic societies—political parties and representative assemblies—have evolved in accordance with the changes in society. In some countries this might mean considering reforms that would make it easier for those in office to take decisions that would have the full authority of the state. In Britain that is not the need. In a country where constitutional processes are heavily biased in favor of government, increased public consent is not likely to be achieved by making those wheels turn still more smoothly and grind more fine. Many aspects of British government need to be examined to see whether they can reflect more accurately the full range of legitimate interests that exist in British society, and can thereby contribute to greater public confidence—an examination that we shall undertake later in this book.

CHAPTER 2

Threats to Social Solidarity: Regional Variation and Ethnic Conflict

It is tempting for outsiders to think of Great Britain as a homogeneous country. They see a densely populated nation, relatively small in area, with a tradition of unitary government. So they tend to refer to the United Kingdom as "England," blithely unaware of the offense this causes to the Scots, the Welsh, and the Northern Irish. Nor are outsiders alone to blame. Walter Bagehot's great work on how Britain was governed a century ago was entitled *The English Constitution,*[1] and is just one of the numerous and apparently trivial examples of the insensitivity that has so often characterized the English attitude toward the other nations that make up the United Kingdom.

To many people, outsiders and English alike, the United Kingdom consists of England plus—with the plus often not figuring large in their minds. Yet the complexity of the relationship is attested by the variety of appellations. The United Kingdom covers England, Wales, Scotland, and Northern Ireland—and from 1801 until the formation of the Irish Free State (now the Republic of Ireland) in 1922, it included the whole of Ireland. Great Britain refers to England, Wales, and Scotland. The British Isles are the two islands of Great Britain and Ireland (the whole of Ireland). England means . . . England.

The visitor is struck by the relatively small number of surnames found among the fifty-five million people of Britain. This lack of variety can lead to no little confusion for those who do not know their way around British institutions, as the British expect.[2] A recent head of the august Social Science Research Council, for example, shares the name Derek Robinson with the former shop steward at British Leyland in Coventry, nicknamed Red Robbo, who led the work stoppages there in 1979. There are the two unrelated Hugh Frasers: Mr. Hugh, M.P., replaced Sir Hugh on the board of Scottish and Universal Investments in connection with a battle in the world of high finance. We have never ascertained the exact number of distinguished gentlemen—all named Michael Stewart—who have had something to do with the conduct of the foreign affairs of Great Britain over the last generation, but circumstantial evidence argues there have been at least three.[3] This situation contrasts with the United States where a population of 220 million seems to have many more than four times the number of surnames that are encountered in Britain, and suggests that, unlike the United States, Britain is to a large extent a handful of extended families.[4] But within the United Kingdom, even within England, a remarkable number of variations are found in a small space. There are northern English prejudices against the south, and southern prejudices against the north—even though these regions are separated by no more than three hundred miles at the most. Numerous local dialects significantly distinguish English people from each other. Even a passing acquaintance with the life and works of Professor Henry Higgins cannot prepare visitors for the rich regional cultures that produce the accents of the West Country or the West Midlands, or Cornish or Yorkshire patriotism.[5]

In the past thirty years a further variation has been introduced into British life with the settlement of more than a million black and brown immigrants from the Commonwealth. This is a drop in the bucket by American standards, but it is enough in Britain to provoke severe social tensions. Nonetheless, it is the relationship of the other nations to England as the dominant partner which has caused particular anxiety about the cohesion, and indeed the preservation, of the United Kingdom. There is nothing new in this condition. For half a century before the First World War, British politics was disrupted by the Irish Question. It was the Irish Question that provoked the first major split in the Liberal party when Joseph Chamberlain broke with William Ewart Gladstone over the first Home Rule Bill in 1886. And it was the Irish Question again that brought the United Kingdom to the brink of civil war just before the outbreak of the First World War in 1914, when feelings ran high as to whether Ulster—the nine northern counties—should be forced into the plan for Irish home rule.[6] The difficulties that have developed over Northern Ireland, Scotland, and Wales in recent years are not a new experience in British politics so much as the reopening of old wounds and the posing once again of familiar questions.

NORTHERN IRELAND

The troubles that have brought such suffering to Northern Ireland over the past decade have their roots deep in history. The conflict is religious, not in the sense that it is centered upon any doctrinal or theological dispute, but only because different religions have become the badges of the two communities that have existed alongside each other for centuries. It is essentially a tribal struggle. The Catholics are the indigenous people of Ireland. The first wave of Protestant settlement came in the later part of the sixteenth century when Elizabeth I awarded land in Ireland to English Protestants as a means of keeping the country under control. This policy was taken further by the Stuart kings, who brought to Ireland a number of Scottish Presbyterians as well as English, and by Cromwell, who also used grants of Irish land as a means of rewarding his soldiers as well as of securing control over Ireland.

Protestantism was the distinguishing feature of the settlers and of their descendants who congregated mostly in the northeast of the island. Inevitably there was a degree of intermarriage with local Catholics, but not so much as might have been expected. The Protestants remained a separate community, more prosperous but not simply a landed elite; they were resented by the Catholics and were, in their turn, resentful of them. Many members of the Protestant community maintained close personal links with Britain, but for most of them Ireland was home. Their roots there go back as far as those of the white Anglo-Saxon Protestants in America. (Had the early American settlers failed to overwhelm the American Indians, their situation would be similar in the United States today.)

In 1800 there was a union of the British and Irish parliaments, and in the late nineteenth century a large majority of the M.P.'s that the Irish sent to the British Parliament at Westminster in London were Nationalists, who were concerned not with the government of the United Kingdom as a whole but with how to exploit their position in the House of Commons in order to achieve their ends for Ireland. In consequence of their efforts, they became such an indigestible element in the British Parliament that one of the motives for support of Prime Minister Gladstone's first Home Rule Bill in 1886 was the prospect of turning the Irish M.P.'s out of Westminster.

This bill was defeated in the Commons; and a second Home Rule Bill was piloted by Gladstone through the Commons, but failed to get through the Lords. A third Home Rule Bill, however, did reach the statute book in 1914. It faced the implacable opposition of the Protestants of Ulster and was not implemented before the outbreak of the First World War. At the time of the first Home Rule Bill, Lord Randolph Churchill, the father of Sir Winston, coined the phrase "Ulster will fight and Ulster will be right." Whether Ulster would have been right then or later was a matter of dispute, but there was every indication that Ulster was still ready to fight in 1914.

This is an example of the bitterness and violence that have disfigured Irish affairs for so long. The Catholic majority, with memories of famine, absentee landlords, coercion, and neglect, were not prepared to remain under the British government.[7] The Protestant minority were not prepared to be ruled by an Irish government representing the Catholic majority. These are the incompatible objectives that still thwart all attempts to secure a peaceful resolution of the Northern Irish problem. In 1914 there was the prospect of civil war in Ireland, with no certainty that the British army would respond to the commands of the British government to put down an Ulster rising if the Protestants of Northern Ireland were to rebel against the home rule scheme.

This crisis was pushed into the background by the outbreak of a wider war. But when the First World War was over, the Lloyd George government was still faced with the Irish conundrum: the Catholics would not accept government from London; the Protestants of the north would not agree to be governed as part of a united Ireland; but the Catholics would not acquiesce in the partition of Ireland. In the attempt to square this circle, Lloyd George devised the Government of Ireland Act of 1920 which provided for two subordinate Irish parliaments within the United Kingdom—one in Dublin for the south of Ireland, and another in Belfast for six of the nine counties of Ulster in the north. In addition, there was to be a Council of Ireland with representatives from the two parliaments of north and south, who were empowered to terminate partition and set up one parliament and government for the whole of Ireland by mutual agreement. The act therefore held out the prospect of a united Ireland, but gave the Ulster Parliament a veto upon any such development.

It was perhaps appropriate that the outcome of such ambiguous legislation should itself be paradoxical. The Catholics in the south would not accept a parliament subordinate to the British Parliament. So the Anglo-Irish Treaty of 1921 was negotiated, providing for the departure of Southern Ireland from the United Kingdom and for the establishment of the Irish Free State, later to be the Republic of Ireland. The Council of Ireland never met. And the only part of the 1920 act that was implemented was the creation of a parliament for the north, where the majority had originally not wanted one and were perfectly content with the existing arrangements whereby they were governed as part of the United Kingdom.

This might nonetheless have proved to be a lasting settlement if partition had neatly divided the two communities. But there remained a minority of Catholics in the north who did not accept that they should be forever part of the United Kingdom, and who looked forward to the reunification of Ireland. With higher living standards in the north, there has for many years been a steady migration of Catholics from the Republic. Their continued presence in the north acts as a perpetual stimulant to the ambition of the south to absorb the north within an enlarged Republic—indeed, it is the justification for that ambition—and has always been a cause of anxiety for Northern Irish Protestants.

The Protestants do not look upon most of the Catholics in Northern Ireland as fellow citizens in the full sense of the term. The Protestants can regard them as social neighbors but not as fellow citizens who are ready to accept the state and the constitution under which they live. The Catholics, for their part, have suffered discrimination in Northern Ireland. These two factors have reinforced each other. Much of the discrimination against Catholics in the north is to be attributed to social prejudice and economic greed. But discrimination in political matters owes a great deal to the fear of Protestants that the Constitution would be undermined if the Catholics had political control, because the latter would use that power to take Northern Ireland out of the United Kingdom. And the more that the Catholics have been discriminated against in Northern Ireland, the more attached they have become to the goal of a united Ireland.

That goal has always been the objective of the Republic, whose government has pursued it by peaceful means, irrespective of party. But such restraint has not been displayed by the terrorists of the Irish Republican Army (IRA), which is an illegal organization in the Republic—though, paradoxically, not in the north, where they do most of their damage. From partition onward there have been waves of IRA violence from time to time in Northern Ireland and occasionally in Britain itself. The era of disorder that has presented such a problem for the United Kingdom in recent years dates from 1968. The pattern has become familiar: civil rights marches by the Catholics and those who sympathize with them as an oppressed minority; counter demonstrations by the Protestants; the marches of one side disrupted by violence from the other; the IRA taking over what had begun as a peaceful protest against discrimination in order to wage a campaign of terror. In due course violent Protestant groups were formed as a counter to the IRA, with members of both the Catholic and the Protestant communities suffering from intimidation at the hands of those who have posed as their protectors.

In the course of this communal violence more than two thousand people have been killed since August 1969, about three quarters of them civilians. Large sums of money have been paid from public funds as compensation for criminal injuries and for criminal damage to property. Especially in the industrial areas of the province, Belfast and Londonderry, bombs in public places and the urban guerrilla's bullet have become regular hazards of life. Merely to walk through the neighborhoods principally affected, to see the shops boarded up and the houses gutted, is to appreciate what a nightmare it has been for the people living there.

The first response of the British government was to send British troops to Northern Ireland in 1969 in an attempt to secure public order. They were welcomed by the Catholics as protectors against Protestant violence and have remained there ever since, though the attitudes of the two communities have now reversed. In March 1972 the Northern Irish Parliament at Stormont, outside Belfast, was abolished by the Heath government in London. Ulster was to be ruled directly from Westminster with William Whitelaw as Secretary of State for Northern Ireland. For just over fifty years the Parliament and the government at Stormont had given Northern Ireland control over most aspects of its internal affairs, with only such matters as foreign policy, defense, overseas trade, the coinage, and some powers of taxation being formally reserved to Westminster. There was also a separate Northern Ireland civil service. To some extent this devolution of governmental authority was always a matter of symbolism rather than of substance—quite apart from the ultimate control retained by Westminster—because Northern Ireland depended upon financial assistance from London if its citizens were to enjoy the same standard of services as people elsewhere in the United Kingdom, and because successive governments in Northern Ireland were so anxious to preserve the union that they voluntarily kept in step with most of the policies being pursued by the British government.

Yet the symbolism mattered for two reasons. The first was that it drew attention to the extent that social life in Northern Ireland is different from that in the rest of the United Kingdom. It emphasized the distinction both to Ulster and to the British people; and, indeed, having their own governmental arrangements did enable the Northern Irish to do a number of things differently even if this never entailed a sharp divergence of policy. Second, the Stormont Parliament came to symbolize for the Catholics the political fact of Protestant control in Northern Ireland. The degree to which the Stormont Parliament was itself an agent of discrimination is in question. There was probably far more discrimination through local government and in social and economic life than through Stormont directly. But the abolition of proportional representation in 1929 for elections to Stormont did encourage the polarization of Ulster politics, which was bound to be damaging to Catholic interests as the minority community.

At all events, whether justified or not, in the minds of the Catholics Stormont had come to represent Protestant oppression. The principal Catholic party of Northern Ireland, the Social Democratic and Labor party (SDLP), withdrew from the Stormont Parliament eight months before it was abolished, and the imposition of direct rule from the British Parliament at Westminster was intended to provide for a new era of nonsectarian government. But direct rule was not designed to be a permanent solution. In June 1973 another Northern Irish assembly was elected under the terms of a new constitution act. This became known as the "power-sharing constitution" because the British government made it a condition of approving the establishment of a new Northern Irish executive that offices would have to be distributed among members of more than one party and of more than one community.

So a coalition was formed among the Unionists—the principal Protestant party led by Brian Faulkner, who had been Prime Minister of Northern Ireland when Stormont was abolished—the SDLP, and the Alliance party, a nonsectarian party that has sought to bridge the gap between the two communities but has never won as much support as well-meaning observers from outside the province would have wished. Before this coalition took office at the beginning of January 1974, there was a conference at Sunningdale in England of representatives from the United Kingdom government, the government of the Republic of Ireland, and the new Executive-designate of Northern Ireland. At this conference it was agreed that there should be a Council of Ireland, with a Council of Ministers from north and south, a secretariat, and a consultative assembly with representatives from the *Dail* in Dublin and the Northern Irish Assembly.

This arrangement amounted to a resurrection of the largely abortive proposals of the 1920 Government of Ireland Act, but with one essential difference. Whereas the 1920 act was designed to lead to home rule for the whole of Ireland within the United Kingdom, the Sunningdale scheme seemed to point toward the unification of Ireland outside the United Kingdom. The Council of Ireland would draw north and south together, but nobody imagined that the Republic would contemplate returning to the United Kingdom.

28

So the Sunningdale settlement was regarded with the deepest suspicion by Protestant opinion. Those moderate Protestant leaders who subscribed to it lost influence with their constituents. Their authority was already weakened by the abolition of Stormont, which had the effect of drawing power within the Protestant community away from the democratically elected political figures who had previously enjoyed the prestige and influence of office, and toward more extreme figures—politicians of a demagogic style, such as the Reverend Ian Paisley, who did not need to hold office to have an effect; and paramilitary groups who did not depend upon legitimate political activity of any kind. This trend proved fatal for the power-sharing experiment. In the few months that it lasted, the Executive worked rather well. The unlikely partners managed to combine better than they and others had expected. But resentment and suspicion within the Protestant community were too great. The hard-liners did well in the United Kingdom general election of February 1974. Indeed, many people believe that the power-sharing experiment was destroyed by the accident of this election following so soon after the experiment had started. Within two months, in May 1974 a general strike in Northern Ireland, fomented by the hard-line Ulster Workers' Council, forced the resignation of the Executive.

This strike, which was accompanied by intimidation in its early stages, soon showed that the Protestant workers had it in their power to bring to a standstill all industrial activity in the province. Northern Irish civil servants and ministers alike concluded that the Executive had no alternative but to resign if the people of Northern Ireland were to be spared intolerable suffering. It was one of the most remarkable examples in any democratic country of a successful political strike, but it brought no nearer a lasting solution to the problems of the province. The search for such a solution has continued without success.

A constitutional convention was elected and sat in 1975 and 1976 without being able to agree on a basis for establishing a new assembly in the province. Other attempts have repeatedly been made to negotiate a political settlement; but they have all foundered partly on the mistrust of centuries and partly on the incompatible aims of the two communities. The Protestants insist upon a new assembly. The Catholics will agree to a new assembly only if it has a power-sharing executive, which the Protestants will not accept. Perhaps it might be different if the conciliatory Alliance party could win a position of greater strength; but so long as power sharing involves cooperating with the SDLP, Protestant politicians know that they would be in danger of being disowned by their own voters for appearing to hand over authority to a party wishing to break the union with Britain. They are perfectly aware that one of the features of Ulster politics over the past decade has been the outflanking of successive Protestant leaders by those who are more extreme and intransigent. The new figures have been not only politicians but also leaders of the Ulster Workers' Council, the Ulster Defense Association, and the Ulster Defense Volunteers.

The Protestants are in a comfortable majority in Northern Ireland, where they include more than half of the population of a million and a half, as against a Catholic community of fewer than one third of the whole population. In the Republic, to the south, there are some three million people, the overwhelming majority of whom are Catholic. So the Protestants would be heavily outnumbered in a united Ireland, where they in their turn would fear discrimination. That, rather than their deep attachment to Britain, of which so much is heard, is no doubt the principal reason that they want to remain part of the United Kingdom. Yet the Catholics never wanted Ireland to be partitioned at all. When the Irish Free State (now the Republic) was created, Catholics in the north wanted to be part of it just as much as did Catholics in the south.

From time to time there are demands, not always couched in delicate political language, that the British government should take a new initiative in Northern Ireland. Such demands often amount in effect to a plan for Britain to start a process that would lead to reunification. The difficulty is what to do about the Protestants. There would be moral and practical objections to expelling people

30

from the nation-state of which they have always been members—and they would have to be expelled if Ireland were to be reunified against their will. It is not the same thing as meeting the wishes of a united country that wants either to be independent or to join another country. From time to time there have been suggestions that Ireland should be repartitioned so as to enable the Catholics of the north to become part of the Republic; but that would be impossible without a major shift of population, because so many Catholics live in the Protestant-dominated industrial areas of Belfast and Londonderry.

Northern Ireland has been part of the United Kingdom for nearly two hundred years. Most of its Protestants wish to remain citizens as they have been throughout that period. At the time of partition the terms of the 1920 act assured them that they could not be forced into a united Ireland without the approval of the Northern Ireland Parliament. When Stormont was abolished in 1972, there was some anxiety in Ulster that this safeguard would be lost; but successive British governments have repeated the guarantee that Northern Ireland would remain part of the United Kingdom so long as that was the wish of a majority of its people. To give force to that assurance, a referendum was held in March 1973: 58 percent of the electorate voted to stay in the United Kingdom, 1 percent voted to join the Republic in a united Ireland, and 41 percent abstained—as they had been encouraged to do by the SDLP. After that poll it is hard to believe that Northern Ireland could be taken out of the United Kingdom without either another referendum or at least a favorable vote in a new Northern Ireland assembly.

Even apart from theoretical majoritarian scruples, there would be the practical difficulty of forcing the majority of Northern Irishmen into a united Ireland against their will. In 1974 the Protestant workers showed their capacity to bring the life of the province to a standstill. There would also be the risk of armed resistance. For nearly a century Britain's Irish policy has been complicated by the fear that Ulster would fight against being taken into a united

Ireland, and there are no solid grounds to think this fear should be any less today. The IRA are not the only hard men in Ireland: the Protestants have their military groups as well.

It has often been suggested that if the British government were to endorse the principle of a united Ireland, and if British troops were to be withdrawn as an indication of that purpose, then the Protestants would be forced to come to terms with the Republic and with the Catholics in their own midst. British withdrawal might have that effect, but it would still more likely lead to a communal bloodbath; and it is understandable that no British government has been prepared to take that chance. It would be a different matter if a majority in the north sought reunification with the south or, more probably, independence. There would be no sufficient reason for a British government to resist either demand. But neither has yet been made.

So the Ulster problem drags on. Under the terms of an act of Parliament passed before the 1979 general election, the number of members from Northern Ireland will increase in the next Parliament from twelve to seventeen to take account of the fact that Northern Ireland no longer has an assembly of its own. But the Catholics are not pleased by anything that can be interpreted as leading to the closer integration of Northern Ireland within the United Kingdom. So this remains a conflict to which there is neither a straightforward solution nor even a promising compromise, given the declared positions of the two sides.

This conflict is distressing for the inhabitants of Northern Ireland, but what of its consequences for the United Kingdom? The Ulster tragedy is part of the bedeviled history of Ireland. Is it equally part of the history of Britain? The answer is yes for two reasons. The first concerns the timing of the outbreak of the present troubles. The two incompatible communities of Ulster have in past time lived side by side more peaceably than in the era of violence that began in 1968. It is surely significant that the increase of violence there coincided with an upsurge of nationalist feeling in Scotland and Wales; and it is not fanciful to see all these developments as in part a recognition of the growing weakness and incapacity of the central authority of the United Kingdom. Each in its own way was a challenge to the increasingly vulnerable center.

Moreover, the Ulster troubles have further weakened British power. There has been the direct additional cost of military operations in Northern Ireland, which is officially calculated to have risen each year since the troubles began to reach a figure of £81.5 million in 1978–79. There has been an indirect impact on the army, whose normal rotation of posting and training has been disrupted by the need to provide troops for a succession of the short tours that are all that even trained soldiers are thought to be able to endure in the conditions of Northern Ireland. This drain on manpower has caused concern among Britain's allies in the North Atlantic Treaty Organization, who are never quite sure whether any British contingent is really free to perform its NATO functions. There has also been the general diversion of British governmental time and energy. The February 1974 general election, for example, which the Heath government lost, might have been held some weeks earlier, with different consequences, if some cabinet ministers had not wished to avoid an election at that time for fear of upsetting the power-sharing experiment in Ulster.[8]

In one respect the Ulster crisis has not been a threat to the United Kingdom. If peace in Northern Ireland could be secured by its departure from the United Kingdom, this is a price that Britain could happily afford to pay. There have in the past been strategic considerations. During the Second World War the Republic not only remained neutral but denied its ports to British vessels. But with both the Republic and Britain now members of the European Community, there would be no reason for Britain to fear the military implications of a united Ireland. The withdrawal of Northern Ireland, if that ever does come about, would not disrupt the United Kingdom economically, politically, or psychologically. Thus, it is very different from Scotland and Wales.[9]

BRITAIN'S POLITICAL AGENDA

DEVOLUTION: SCOTLAND AND WALES

One of the most remarkable episodes in recent British political history was the attempt to assuage what was assumed to be the constitutional restlessness of the Scots and the Welsh. In the years immediately following the general elections of 1974 there was much anxiety about whether Scotland in particular could be kept within the United Kingdom. The Scottish National party, who were and are committed to the creation of an independent Scottish state, won 30 percent of the total vote in Scotland at the October 1974 election. Because in the British electoral system members of Parliament are elected on a plurality—that is, on a first-past-the-post basis—they won no more than eleven of the seventy-one Scottish seats. They came in second for thirty-six seats, however, and were poised to capture a majority of these seats if they could secure even a small increase in their share of the poll.

The possibility of a constitutional crisis became evident. If the Scots were ever to break away, this would be a grave matter for the rest of the United Kingdom. It is not simply that Scotland is a larger country than the province of Northern Ireland and has a population of nearly six million compared with the latter's one and one-half million. In social and economic life Scotland has been more closely entwined with England. Most of what is now known as British oil lies beneath what would become Scottish waters, however defined by international law, if Scotland were to be an independent state. The United Kingdom's standing internationally, and especially within the European Community, would suffer if it no longer included Scotland. A separation would also seem to provide—indeed, it would provide—confirmation of the disintegration of Britain. British trade might be damaged at home and overseas. And it would certainly be a severe blow to English self-confidence. All these results would occur with almost equal force if Wales were to leave the United Kingdom, with the exception of the factor of oil, which has not yet been found off the Welsh coast.

The House of Commons devoted the best part of two parliamentary sessions, in 1976–77 and 1977–78, to the examination of bills providing for Scottish and Welsh devolution, consisting of subordinate parliamentary assemblies for Scotland and Wales within the United Kingdom. Eventually the legislation was passed, though not with any enthusiasm. There was never a majority of M.P.'s who positively favored it. Enough of them went along with it either because of pressure from the Labour government's party managers, or because they thought it was necessary to undercut Nationalist party support, or to meet the aspirations of the Scots and the Welsh and thereby keep them in the United Kingdom. Then, in the referendums, which Parliament had decided must be held before the assemblies were brought into being, the Welsh voted overwhelmingly against the scheme, and the Scots approved it by too narrow a majority for its execution to be politically feasible.

Devolution was killed by the Scots and the Welsh themselves. Was this because of the numerous defects in the particular plans that the government put forward? Had the Scots and the Welsh changed their minds? Had they never been so restless as the politicians had supposed? Or was there another explanation?

The history of the relationship of Scotland to England is different from that of Wales, and both of them differ still more from the experience of Northern Ireland. At no time in its history has Northern Ireland been a separate nation. It is a province, whereas Scotland and Wales are historic nations. Wales has not been governed as a separate nation for centuries. Scotland, on the other hand, had its own monarchy until the union of the crowns in 1603, and its own parliament until the parliaments were united by treaty in 1707. By British standards, this is almost within living memory. A visitor can engage a cab in Edinburgh and say to the driver, "Take me to Parliament House." The driver will know not only where to go but also why Parliament House bears that title. It is symbolism such as this that reminds the Scots that they used to govern themselves.

Nor is it only a matter of symbolism. The Scots have retained their own national church, their own legal system, their own civil law, and their own schools. They have had their own law officers in the government since the Treaty of Union in 1707. There has been a Secretary for Scotland with a separate Scottish Office since Lord Rosebery bullied Prime Minister Gladstone to make this concession to Scottish pride in 1885. In 1926 the Scottish Secretary was raised to the status of Secretary of State, with a seat in the Cabinet; and since 1939 there has been a Scottish Office in Edinburgh as well as in London. Over the years a wide range of responsibilities has been devolved to the Scottish Office—from housing, health, and schools to agriculture and economic development—so that it is generally agreed that there is little room to devolve the public administration of Scotland much further. The distinctive Scottish legal system has also required that a certain amount of separate legislation for Scotland should be passed by the Westminster Parliament. It is evident, in short, that the much-trumpeted unitary system of British government has accommodated substantial exceptions.

This complexity of government has been matched by a certain ambiguity of Scottish attitudes toward the United Kingdom. Throughout the period that Scotland has been part of the United Kingdom, ruled by the British Parliament at Westminster, there has remained a distinctive feeling of Scottish social identity. Scots have been aware of a double loyalty, which has not stopped them from playing an active part in the conduct of British affairs, governmental and otherwise. The feeling of being Scottish has been merged in the wider loyalty not just of the United Kingdom but of the British Empire. This was partly because the Scottish educational system is more highly developed than the English, with a higher proportion of bright Scottish children of all social classes going on from school to university. With so many graduates in a small country, it was not surprising that many of them looked outside Scotland for appropriate careers.

The loss of empire and the general contraction of British horizons has therefore been disturbing to the Scots. It is one thing to play a leading part in managing the British Empire, but quite another to be annexed to little England. In the past the Scots were associated with an enterprise that was regarded as successful. In recent years they have found themselves in partnership with what is widely seen as a failure. For the ambitious Scot, England used to be the big time. Now it seems to be the place where they make a mess of things.

Such considerations have much to do with disenchantment in Scotland with the United Kingdom. Some of them apply to Wales as well, but with less force. Since Wales has not been governed as a separate entity for many centuries, its national institutions have not been preserved in the same way. Its sense of identity is not so assured. There is also a matter of geography: north and south Wales have in many ways more in common with the neighboring parts of England than with each other. Administrative devolution has also come more slowly to Wales than to Scotland. It was not until 1951 that there was a cabinet minister with special responsibility for Welsh affairs, and then it was the home secretary who was simply given Wales as an added task. Wales had to wait another thirteen years before it had a cabinet minister of its own and a Welsh Office with administrative duties, though since then the Welsh have been catching up with the Scots on administrative devolution.

These differences have much to do with the distinction between Scottish and Welsh nationalism. The Welsh variety is largely a cultural nationalism, concerned above all with the preservation of the Welsh language and village way of life, even though it has its political objectives. Scottish nationalism, on the other hand, gives absolute priority to political and economic purposes. The rise of both in the 1960s and 1970s was linked to the decline in Britain's fortunes.

The Scottish Nationalists first won a seat in Parliament at a by-election in 1945, but then lost it at the general election a few months later. Then in July 1966, Gwynfor Evans, the president of

Plaid Cymru, the Welsh Nationalists, won a by-election at Car-
marthen. In November the following year, Winifred Ewing won a
by-election for the Scottish National party at Hamilton; and in
1968 the Scottish Nationalists did well in local elections. Both in
Scotland and in Wales, Nationalists seemed to be on the march. It
was also in 1968, it will be recalled, that the most recent round of
troubles began in Northern Ireland. This was the year after the
devaluation of the pound. The Wilson government was doing exceptionally badly in parliamentary by-elections and local elections,
and presented the spectacle of the weakest British administration
within memory.

It was a time of general disillusionment. Economic weakness was
forcing Britain to withdraw from what remained of its traditional
role in both the Far East and the Middle East. It had been rebuffed
a second time by Charles de Gaulle in its attempt to join the
European Community. The rise of nationalism in Scotland and
Wales, with the accompanying threat of ultimate secession from
the United Kingdom, both was partly caused by this sense of
British fallibility and served to compound it.

The Conservatives responded to this upsurge of nationalist feeling by what became known as Mr. Heath's "Declaration of Perth"
when, as leader of the party at the 1968 conference of Scottish
Conservatives, he came out in favor of the principle of a Scottish
assembly, whose proposed powers were to be defined by a committee that he appointed under the chairmanship of Sir Alec Douglas-
Home, the former Prime Minister who was to be Foreign Secretary
again from 1970 to 1974. The Labour government's response was
to appoint a Royal Commission on the Constitution.

Both major parties thus sought to defuse nationalism by going
part of the way to meet its demands. There was already in existence
a body of thought that favored the devolution of power from
Westminster on grounds of good government.[10] The creation of
regional assemblies, subordinate to Westminster, would, it was
maintained, be democratically healthy because it would bring the

process of decision making closer to the people affected by policies. Government would no longer seem so faceless, remote, and insensitive.

Some of those who took this view wanted a full-blown federal system, with the powers of each level of government defined in law and enforceable by the courts. Some wanted a pattern of regional government throughout Great Britain, but with the British Parliament retaining both the ultimate authority and the power to intervene on particular policy questions if it chose to do so. Others wanted a devolved form of government for Scotland and Wales alone, or simply for Scotland. And a good many were muddled about precisely what form of regional government they wanted.

All these points of view were in due course reflected in the Royal Commission report, with one exception: It ruled out federalism in the sense of regional assemblies with reserved powers constitutionally determined.[11] There were many divisions within the commission, but the majority favored directly elected assemblies for Scotland and Wales with the power to legislate over a range of social and industrial matters, while maintaining the supremacy of Parliament. A separate minority report proposed similar assemblies for Scotland, Wales, and five regions of England, with executive but not legislative powers.[12]

The most ardent advocates of devolution believed in it as a superior form of government: that was why some of the most persuasive of them wanted to apply it to the regions of England as well, where there was no nationalist threat to be neutralized. But the major parties were not interested in it for this reason; rather, they saw it only as a means of undermining the nationalist parties. That was why the Heath government did nothing about devolution from 1970 to 1974, even though the Douglas-Home committee had reported early in 1970 in favor of a directly elected Scottish assembly that would process some stages of purely Scottish bills before returning them for the final approval of the Westminster Parliament. When the Scottish National party failed to maintain its momentum at the 1970 general election, losing the seat it had but gaining another, and *Plaid Cymru* lost its only seat, the government, amidst all its other anxieties, felt able to forget about Scotland and Wales. And when the Royal Commission report was published in October 1973, it was received by a distinctly bored House of Commons.

In the February 1974 election the Scottish Nationalists won seven seats, and Plaid Cymru, two. In the October election of that year the Scottish National Party (SNP) advanced to eleven seats and 30 percent of the total Scottish poll, and the Welsh Nationalists had three seats. Boredom in the major parties was succeeded by alarm. How could the United Kingdom be preserved? Between these two elections the issue of nationalism vaulted to the top of the political agenda. In the October election the Labour government, which was returned to office as a minority administration in February and now had a small majority, set out to redeem its promise.

The task was complicated because, although Labour leaders had accepted devolution as a political necessity and had indeed pressed the policy upon a hesitant Labour party in Scotland, the implications for the British system of government had not been thought through. Many members of the Cabinet seemed barely aware that a commitment had been made. In the light of future events, it was significant that among the most reluctant to proceed was James Callaghan, then Foreign Secretary. The policy might well have been sunk by this evident lack of enthusiasm had it not been for the still more evident challenge of the Nationalists.

After their success in the October 1974 election, the Nationalists for a time went from strength to strength in Scotland. They became the leading party in the opinion polls and triumphed in local by-elections. Had there been another general election within a few months, it appeared that they would win more than half the Scottish seats, which they had always proclaimed would be a mandate to establish an independent Scotland. Even if that claim was not granted, there would in those circumstances have been a major constitutional crisis. The Nationalists were helped by the discovery of oil in large quantities in the North Sea, which suddenly multiplied in value after the Yom Kippur War of 1973. Many Scots who were romantic and sentimental nationalists had always believed that no canny, sensible person could afford separation from England. That materialist consideration was suddenly stood on its head by the argument that if only Scotland was independent, most of the oil would fall under the jurisdiction of the Scottish government.

Nonetheless, supporters of independence never amounted to more than 30 percent of the Scottish people at the very most.[13] That level of support lasted only briefly, and paradoxically not all those who voted independence favored Nationalist. The Nationalists drew many of their voters from two other groups. One was what might be termed the Scottish assertion vote: those who wanted a greater recognition of Scottish identity, a better deal for Scotland, without leaving the United Kingdom. The other group was the protest vote: those people who wished to register their dissatisfaction with both the main British parties and in England would have voted Liberal in order to do so. In Scotland the SNP seemed a more positive and glamorous home for these protesters. Voting for the SNP was a good way of kicking the shins of whoever was in office in London.

The political purpose of devolution was to siphon off this second- and third-line support for the SNP by meeting Scotland's distinctive needs within the United Kingdom, in particular by providing a constitutional recognition of Scottish identity which would stop short of independence. The Nationalists are at their strongest when they are able to argue convincingly that there are other reasons for supporting them apart from the pursuit of independence: "Even if you don't want independence, a vote for the SNP will strengthen the voice of Scotland." The more it could be shown that there was no other credible reason for voting for the party apart from seeking independence, the weaker its electoral appeal was likely to be.

That was the political rationale for giving devolution to Scotland. The case for Wales was by the mid-1970s much weaker: after their breakthrough in 1966 the Welsh Nationalists had not made the same advance as had the Nationalists in Scotland. The danger of Wales leaving the United Kingdom seemed remote. There remained only a feeling that if Scotland was to have an assembly, something must be done for Wales. Devolution had for some years been the official policy of the Labour party in Wales; and there were many public bodies responsible for important activities there, run by officially nominated boards, which it was thought desirable to bring under direct democratic control. An assembly, it was believed, could do this.

So a scheme was devised to give Scotland an assembly with legislative and executive powers over a wide range of essentially social matters—health, housing, schools, and so forth—and to give Wales an assembly with purely executive responsibilities in much the same fields. This scheme was embodied in the Scotland and Wales Bill that was presented to Parliament toward the end of 1976. It met with much criticism for a number of reasons. Many M.P.'s did not like the idea of parliamentary devolution at all; some English members were insensitive to the special interests of the Scots and the Welsh. Many also feared the break-up of the United Kingdom. There was much talk of the undesirability of treading upon what might become a slippery slope to independence and of the impossibility of basing a lasting constitutional arrangement upon a compromise embracing many logical flaws.

One of the principal flaws, in terms of logic though not of politics, was that the scheme did not propose a uniform method of government for all the different parts of the United Kingdom. Scotland was to have one kind of assembly; Wales, another. Northern Ireland might have an assembly again, but not yet. And England was not to have any separate assemblies at all. There were good political reasons for these differences. There was no strong demand for English regional assemblies and consequently no disposition at Westminster to mess about with the government of

England to suit the convenience of the Scots. Northern Ireland could not for the time being be given another assembly without internal conflict, and the strength of national feeling there was very different from that in Scotland and Wales. The effect was that after this reform the government of the United Kingdom would look considerably more lopsided, asymmetrical, and constitutionally untidy than before.

The lack of uniformity had other practical consequences as well. It made it more difficult to devise satisfactory financial arrangements. The government could not discover forms of taxation that would bring in a sizable amount of money and could be assigned to the assemblies without excessive disruption and expense. So the proposed assemblies were empowered to spend money allocated by London but not to raise any themselves. Opponents of the scheme thus feared that the Scots would forever be complaining that they were starved of funds by the parsimonious English.

Another asymmetry had perplexed Gladstone over Irish home rule nearly a century ago. If part of the United Kingdom was to have a subordinate parliament of its own, should it still be represented at Westminster? Gladstone had toyed with the idea of either excluding the Irish M.P.'s altogether or of allowing them to take part only when Irish or imperial business was being discussed—the so-called in-and-out principle.[14] Neither of these possibilities was proposed for contemporary Scotland for very good reasons. The in-and-out idea would be just as unworkable for the Scots as it would have been for the Irish; and it would have been quite unacceptable to kick all the Scottish M.P.'s out of the Westminster Parliament when such matters of general concern as the economy, foreign affairs, defense, and public order were not to be devolved.

Thus, there would be an anomaly: Scottish M.P.'s would be able to vote on social policies for England, although English M.P.'s would not be able to vote on those policies for Scotland. In practice, English M.P.'s have never shown a lively interest in Scottish social policy, and so they would hardly have felt deprived in any substantive sense. Moreover, precisely the same anomaly existed in the case of Northern Ireland so long as there was an assembly at Stormont. The difference was that the number of Northern Irish M.P.'s was deliberately kept down to twelve because Ulster had its own assembly—and the act to increase that number was passed in 1979 only when there was no immediate prospect of the assembly being restored. Consequently, the Northern Irish never held the balance of power at Westminster. Had they done so, there might indeed have been resentment at the anomaly, as there would have been with seventy-one Scottish members.

Why, then, not reduce their numbers as the Royal Commission on the Constitution suggested?[15] Because that would sharply diminish Labour's chances of forming the government at Westminster in the future. Labour's hopes of having a majority in the House of Commons generally depend upon winning most of the Scottish seats.[16] Throughout the consideration of devolution the Labour government was taunted with the charge of being concerned only with saving the party's electoral skin in Scotland. In one sense the accusation was beside the point. The Nationalists could win a majority of the Scottish seats only by taking a good number from Labour.[17] So what was good for preserving the United Kingdom was also bound to be good for Labour. But the government went further in securing its own party interest; and in order to do so, it was even prepared to damage the prospects for the acceptable working of the devolution scheme. The refusal to reduce the number of Scottish seats was one example. The rejection of proportional representation for the assemblies was another. With a proportional system of election there would be no risk of the Nationalists slipping into power without the support of a majority of voters, and consequently there would be less danger of the slippery slope to independence. Both Labour and the Conservatives were afraid, however, of setting a precedent for Westminster elections, which would be contrary to their party interests. So they refused to have proportional representation for the assemblies.

The government's first attempt, the Scotland and Wales Bill, was killed by a procedural vote in the House of Commons in February

1976. The following session two separate bills were introduced: one each for Scotland and for Wales. This made sense because two different forms of devolution were proposed. The division of powers between the respective assemblies and the Westminster Parliament was also drawn more clearly, though there was still a great deal of complexity and confusion about who would be responsible for what. Eventually a reluctant Parliament passed the bills, but only after two critical changes from the government's original intentions were made. In order to appease its parliamentary critics, the government itself proposed that before the assemblies could be set up there should be advisory referendums of the electorates in both Scotland and Wales. In either country, if there was a majority against an assembly, the government agreed to place an order before Parliament to repeal the act. The House of Commons, in other words, would have to vote again before the legislation could either be implemented or repealed. The House could act in the light of the referendums but without being required to accept their results. While these bills were going through the House, an independent-minded Labour backbencher, George Cunningham, managed to have amendments passed requiring the Secretary of State to place an order for repeal if the majority in favor of an assembly was less than 40 percent of those entitled to vote—leaving the Commons the authority to form its own judgment.

In Wales only a derisory 12 percent voted for devolution. The 40 percent provision turned out to be crucial for Scotland, where 33 percent of the electorate voted for devolution, 31 percent voted against, and 36 percent did not bother to vote at all. In these circumstances, where abstainers could be represented as voting against devolution because of the 40 percent rule, there was no chance of the Commons voting to go ahead with the assembly. The government knew this well enough and delayed introducing any order, which provoked the Nationalists to vote with the Conservatives so as to bring down the government and to precipitate the election of May 1979. With the Conservatives returned to power, and with the Scottish and Welsh Nationalists reduced to two members each, the repeal of the acts was a mere formality in the new Parliament. Devolution was dead.

The whole story is a curious episode in British political history. The strength of national feeling in Wales was probably exaggerated by those who looked at what was happening in Scotland and assumed that the Welsh would follow. But why did the Scots fail to vote in sufficient numbers for a reform that a large majority had earlier been shown by the opinion polls to favor? Why did the 30 percent of Scottish votes for the SNP in October 1974 melt away to a mere 17 percent in the general election of 1979? To anybody watching the Scottish scene at close hand, it was evident that the steam progressively went out of the Scottish issue during 1978 and 1979. The devolution scheme was complicated, people were confused, and they were told by some Conservatives that, if they rejected this version, they would have the chance later of approving a superior model. The prospect of an extra tier of government fed fears of over-government and the waste of public money: in that sense the anti-devolution vote was Scotland's Proposition 13. The slippery slope argument bit ever more deeply, revealing Scottish anxieties about actually breaking away from England. The anti-devolution case was presented with force and conviction, most notably by Tam Dalyell, Labour M.P. for West Lothian, who waged a remarkable campaign against devolution both in Parliament and in Scotland; whereas the case for the scheme was put either by Nationalists, whose motives were suspect, or by Labour spokesmen, who were too evidently concerned only with political maneuver.[18]

There was still another reason for the change of heart in Scotland —which tells a great deal about the relationship of Scotland to the United Kingdom. Scottish national feeling was defused by the mere offer of an assembly. That Parliament should spend the better part of two sessions discussing various devolution bills was evidence that it took Scotland seriously. Scottish resentment was assuaged. This episode thus offers the United Kingdom not only consolation but a warning. The Scots are a touchy people. They are evidently

46

concerned more about their dignity than about their constitution. So long as leaders and institutions of the United Kingdom can meet that need, sentiment for separatism is likely to be uninfluential. But to believe that the devolution episode was a waste of time, and that it was pointless to pay heed to Scottish sensibilities, is to court another upsurge of nationalism and to threaten the stability of the United Kingdom.

IMMIGRATION AND RACE

A further disturbance to the homogeneity of the United Kingdom has been the influx of Commonwealth immigrants during the post-war years. This has given Britain a racial problem for the first time in its history. Britain is not, as the United States is, a nation of immigrants. There have, it is true, been a number of substantial migrations into Britain in the course of its history. There were the French and Flemish Huguenots, who were refugees from religious persecution in the seventeenth century; Jewish refugees from Russia and Poland at the end of the nineteenth century; Poles and other East Europeans at the end of the Second World War; Hungarian refugees after the 1956 uprising; and the largest inflow of all, the Irish, who have come into Britain in considerable numbers down through the years.

Immigration from what is termed the "New Commonwealth" differs from all of these because it consists for the most part of non-whites, who are less likely to merge into the rest of the population than are most of the other groups.[19] This community is to be distinguished from the American black community in that black Americans have lived in the United States since before the adoption of its Constitution. This distinction is of great importance for race relations in the two countries. In the United States black inhabitants have, as it were, been there always. In Britain the black and brown communities have suddenly appeared as a result of recent immigration. So in Britain the questions of race and of immigration control are linked in a way that they are not in the United States.

Before the Second World War there were small communities of colored people in the ports, particularly in Liverpool and Cardiff, who had been there for a couple of centuries. During the war West Indians were brought over to England to help with the labor shortage in British factories. When peace came, they went back home; but there was much unemployment in the West Indies, and the attractions of Britain beckoned to them and to those who had heard stories of employment there. It was only after migration from the West Indies to the United States was restricted in 1952 that the flow to Britain sharply increased.

It was also in the 1950s that Indian and Pakistani immigrants began moving to Britain in any numbers. They were largely those who had lost their homes in the violence following the partition of the subcontinent between India and Pakistan in 1947, and from among those suffering from a shortage of land in agricultural areas.

The British response was initially favorable. Many of the immigrants—West Indian, Indian, and Pakistani—had been deliberately recruited by British employers. London Transport, for example, had a scheme to recruit workers from Barbados for the Underground. Immigrants were often a source of cheap labor and were prepared to do the kind of work for which it was difficult to find British employees. There was also a feeling that one of the obligations of leadership in the Empire and the Commonwealth was to offer an open door to anyone from any member country. Just as anyone anywhere in the Roman Empire was a citizen of Rome, so anyone from any part of the British Commonwealth should be free to come to Britain.

These high-minded principles began to be challenged as social tensions developed between the immigrants and their closest neighbors in the areas where they congregated. There are now probably fewer than two million colored people in Britain, about one in thirty of the total population. This is not a racial mixture anywhere near approximating the proportion of black people in the United States, who make up between one tenth and one ninth of the American population; and by American standards the associated problems seem so trivial as to underscore fundamentally tribal aspects of the larger British populace. The immigrants are not evenly distributed throughout the United Kingdom. Immigrants the world over, of whatever race or color, naturally collect together when they come into a new country. This they have done in Britain. There are particular areas of the country where the proportion of black or Asian people is very much larger than one would gather from overall national statistics—in the northern and midland towns of Bradford, Wolverhampton, and Leicester or the London boroughs of Southall and Brixton. Social tensions have developed in these areas: instances of discrimination in housing and employment, the harassment of members of the minority groups, and instances of physical violence especially by groups of unemployed teen-agers, both colored and white.

As resentments grew, so the pressure to restrict immigration from the Commonwealth began to build up in the late 1950s; and in 1962 the Commonwealth Immigrants Act was passed. This legislation, the first to remove the automatic right of Commonwealth citizens to settle in Britain, was strongly opposed by the Labour party leadership in Parliament. No subsequent government, however, Labour or Conservative, has dared to relax immigration control. Indeed, the trend has been all in the opposite direction. The regulations under the act were considerably tightened in 1965, when it was decided that unskilled workers with no specific job awaiting them would no longer be allowed to enter.

In 1968 a further restriction was imposed when another Commonwealth Immigrants Act applied immigration controls to United Kingdom passport holders who had no connection by birth or family with Britain. The purpose of this act was to prevent the arrival of a flood of Asians with British passports from East African countries as those countries intensified their policy of "Africanization." This prospect presented the British government with a delicate problem. During the independence negotiations for Kenya, Uganda, and Tanzania in the early 1960s, the Asian populations of these African countries were concerned about what would happen to them when Africans began ruling there. They therefore sought and obtained the assurance that they would always have the right to settle in Britain as United Kingdom passport holders. Because they had United Kingdom passports, or the right to have them, many of these people decided not to become citizens of the country in which they were living. Britain had a strong moral as well as legal obligation to them, and the 1968 act was bitterly criticized at home and abroad; but at least it did not withdraw their right to settle in Britain. It simply phased their entry over a period of years through yearly quotas.

Another act in 1971 was designed to tighten immigration control still further. But there remained a dilemma for policy makers. The restrictions on legal immigration were stringent. Most of those entering the United Kingdom legally were either dependents of people already there or were about to marry someone settled there —apart from the East African Asians, who were admitted under a special quota. The scope for further restrictions was limited unless there was to be a deliberate policy to keep members of the same family apart. There has for many years also been a certain amount of illegal immigration—nobody can be sure exactly how much; and it was unlikely to be diminished by further limitation of legal entry. But the public remained largely unappeased, failing to appreciate how far controls had already been applied.

In 1978, while still the leader of the parliamentary opposition, Margaret Thatcher spoke of the fears that many people had of being swamped by immigrants.[20] She was strongly attacked for her provocative and insensitive use of words, which gave the impression that she was not just describing prejudice but defending it. Her motives were also suspect as she was thought to be seeking to take political advantage of the anti-immigrant sentiments of many traditional Labour supporters. She did, however, reflect the fears of many people, especially in neighborhoods that were being transformed by what seemed to locals an endless inflow of black and Asian immigrants—even though legal immigration had been severely restricted for years. These locals craved the assurance that the flow would stop before there was any question of their looking with tolerance on the immigrants already in Britain. The Conservative government that took office in May 1979 introduced new restrictions before the end of the year. The most important of these was to remove the right of women to bring their husbands and fiancés into the country—though women born in Britain would still be permitted to do so as a general rule through the exercise of administrative discretion.

The purpose of this change was to cope with a deliberate evasion of the existing immigration controls. The Asian custom of the arranged marriage was being used to enable a small but increasing number of young men from the Indian subcontinent to settle in Britain. In order to be allowed to do so, they were marrying Asian girls from Britain whom in many instances they had never met. An active trade along those lines was building up, with Asian girls in Britain being offered in marriage to bidders from the subcontinent. It was in accordance with the Asian practice for marriages to be arranged by the families rather than to be the consequence of romantic love—though in Asia it is the custom for the woman to go to the home of the man, not the other way around. It was clearly —by British standards—not abusing the rights of the family or the feelings of individuals to prevent two people who had never met each other from living together in Britain. To that extent this change in the immigration rules was defensible. It was bitterly and justifiably criticized, however, because it discriminated against the rights of women, was almost certainly an infringement of the European Convention on Human Rights, and was obviously designed to prevent more men from the Indian subcontinent from entering Britain, but was likely to be relatively ineffective as a steadily increasing proportion of young Asian women in Britain have been born in the United Kingdom and hence maintain their right to

51

import a husband. It was therefore likely to cause the maximum aggravation for the minimum result.

Nonetheless, in the climate of British opinion tight immigration control is nearly universally regarded as a necessary condition for good race relations.[21] This is true whether the politician's or observer's primary concern is the furtherance of interracial harmony or the exploitation of underlying fears and prejudices. In a worldwide context of racial, ethnic, and tribal standoffishness, if not hostility, this does not seem remarkable. Some of the initial difficulty for Britain came about because of the intolerance of newly emerging African nations for their minorities of Asian descent. Britons can look abroad and note the invention by several of their European neighbors of the anomalous category of "guest worker" —a status assigned to temporary immigrants from less prosperous countries who are needed to do work that the well-off indigenous labor force will no longer do, but who are prevented from obtaining the rights of full-fledged citizens; or they can look to the United States and its long-time immigration restrictions on southern Europeans and Orientals.

British politicians divide on whether it is possible to accommodate to the racial minorities in the numbers already present. Small splinter parties, with avid followers but not seats in Parliament, such as the National Front, base their appeal largely upon race hatred. Somewhat more respectable extremists, like the brilliant eccentric Ulster Unionist M.P., Enoch Powell, formerly a leader of the Conservative right wing, have argued for such measures as "voluntary" subsidized repatriation.

It is difficult to treat such proposals seriously, since they manifestly have so few takers among the sections of the population upon whom it is wished to shower this particular manifestation of the nation's largesse, and also because the narrow tribalism of Englishmen in which such proposals are grounded seems so unlikely a foundation for the policies of a civilized modern democratic nation.

Preventing immigration is not in itself to be regarded as a policy for good race relations. From 1965 on there has been legislation against racial discrimination in Britain. It is unlawful to discriminate on grounds of race against anyone in the provision of services to the public, in housing, or in employment. The Commission for Racial Equality is charged with the task both of enforcing the law and of encouraging good relations among the races in Britain. But it would be an exaggeration to claim that this system works any more than moderately well. The purpose of the law can only be to remove, or at least to reduce, specific impediments in the way of people belonging to racial minorities finding a place for themselves in British society. Yet even this purpose has been by no means fully achieved because of the racial prejudice that unquestionably exists in British society. It is probably no worse in Britain than in other countries with racial variety in their populations; but it is there, and public policy has to take account of it. That is the rationale for a tight immigration policy. To acknowledge the existence of racial prejudice is not, however, to justify it. It undermines British society in two ways. In the first place, it directly threatens social stability, and even public order, in some places. Second, the minority communities can be made scapegoats for the poor performance of the white majority. The production of false alibis is the mark of a nation in decline. Until Britain goes beyond its dreary argument over immigration control and tackles racial discrimination and prejudice more effectively than it has yet done, British society will not be healthy. This is a task that requires the leadership of government, but it cannot be accomplished by government alone.

CHAPTER 3

Managing Shrinkage in World Influence

There are only two superpowers in the world, and Britain is not one of them. To Americans, this will seem a statement of the obvious. To many British people, it sums up their decline in national status. Britain is to be distinguished from such countries as Canada and Brazil in that it has become a middle-sized power through shrinkage, not through growth. It has not—unlike France, Germany, or Japan—had to recover from the humiliation of military defeat. It has suffered the rather different, but no less real, stresses of a progressive decline from a position of international eminence and respect.

To some extent this decline was the natural consequence of economic weakness. "If only I had fifty million tons of coal to export," Ernest Bevin is reported to have lamented time and again while he was foreign secretary in the early postwar years, "what a difference that would make to my foreign policy." No country can expect to have a great impact on international affairs, especially in the world of today where economic considerations matter so much, when it has to be bailed out every now and then by the International Monetary Fund. It is even harder for a country to cut a figure in the world when there is a widespread belief that its economic misfortunes are largely its own fault.

No matter how successful Britain's economic performance over the past thirty-five years, though, it would have been impossible for the United Kingdom to have sustained the international position it enjoyed at the end of the Second World War. At the summit conferences of those days—Teheran, Yalta, Potsdam—the British Prime Minister had an automatic place along with the President of the United States and the leader of the Soviet Union. Yet, even then, this was an unnatural eminence, to be attributed to Britain's record as the one country to have fought throughout the entire war against Nazi Germany, rather than to any estimation of its current power. This reality was not fully appreciated by most British people at that time. Certainly, at the beginning, the wartime partnership was regarded by the British public as an alliance between equals: the United States had the men and the armaments; Britain had the military experience and expertise. This impression was fostered by the formalities of wartime consultation—not just the historic meetings between Roosevelt and Churchill, but also the discussions among military commanders. But Britain could not hope to continue dealing with the Soviet Union and the United States on a basis of apparent equality once the habits and the sentiments of wartime had passed. Not since the Geneva Conference of 1955 has a British prime minister sat down together with the leaders of the two superpowers; and in 1955, France was present as well. The U-2 incident aborted the next planned meeting in 1960. When the American spy plane was shot down over the Soviet Union a few days before the conference was due to begin, Soviet leader Nikita Khrushchev refused to take part. For some time after that canceled summit the British were preoccupied with maintaining a place at the top table; but it seems to have been tacitly recognized for some time now that the table has room only for two. The concern these days, not just of Britain but of all the European allies of the United States, is that their interests may be overlooked by the latter in its dealing with the Soviet Union.

FROM EMPIRE TO COMMONWEALTH

At the end of the Second World War, Britain not only had an assured place at the top table but had its empire intact. Or so it seemed. The Statute of Westminster in 1931 had proclaimed that Britain and the dominions were "autonomous communities within the British Empire." These communities were, however, only the old white dominions; and their largely united response during the war blurred the questions that the statute had posed. "I have not become the King's First Minister in order to preside over the liquidation of the British Empire," Churchill declared in 1942. By the time Churchill returned as Prime Minister in 1951, the decisive step toward that liquidation, the independence of India, had been taken without his outright opposition—despite his record as an opponent of the Government of India Act of 1935 and his position in 1947 as the official Leader of the Opposition. The independence of India was not accomplished without bloodshed: more than half a million people were killed in communal violence attending the withdrawal of British authority and the partition of the sub continent into the nations of India and Pakistan. Britain was criticized for the abruptness with which Prime Minister Attlee's government finally decided to withdraw; but at least it voluntarily handed over power in India and thus was able to maintain a bond with these new nations.

Exactly when the Empire evolved into the Commonwealth is worthy of a study in itself, in its way a tribute to the British preference for flexibility rather than for precision in constitutional matters.[1] What is clear is that the emergence of India, Pakistan, and Ceylon as independent members of the Commonwealth, and the dropping of the word "British" from its title in 1949, were historic landmarks. Ghana and Malaysia followed suit in 1957; and from then on most of the remaining British colonies in Africa, Asia, the Carribbean, and the Mediterranean moved toward independence. Today, a little over three decades since the process of disengagement began, there are forty-one full members of the Commonwealth apart from the United Kingdom, all of them independent nations formerly under British rule.

Nobody looking at the arrangements that were made or at the commitments given at the time, or at what has happened subsequently in these countries, could possibly claim that the process was uniformly successful. It was nonetheless a remarkable accomplishment. The great danger when any empire comes to the point where the material basis for its continuation no longer exists is the temptation to continue in the old way. What was important and valuable about the British dismantling of empire was that Britain recognized the signs in time.

The process was aided psychologically for the British public by their belief that Britain was not so much losing an empire as gaining a commonwealth. The development of the modern Commonwealth was partly an emotional crutch for Britain, partly an attempt to devise a mechanism for the continued cooperation with the mother country that would be desirable in many fields for nations that had been so closely tied with Britain over many years, and partly an exercise in creating a new form of international cooperation.

There was a widespread belief in the 1950s and 1960s that this new kind of international partnership, without the forced bonds of empire, was going to be an example that might be duplicated in other instances. Without any member's dominating the combination or being responsible for the internal affairs of any other member, this entirely voluntary relationship of countries on different continents and consisting of peoples with very different backgrounds was, and has remained, unique.

It soon became evident, however, that the Commonwealth has the weaknesses of its own merits. One of its advantages is the extent to which it brings together not only peoples of different races and cultures but also nations whose international policies and commitments are very different—nations that are not aligned, that are members of NATO, that are outside NATO but have alliances with NATO members, and other nations that do not belong in any way to the Western alliance but are broadly favorable to it. Commonwealth membership, therefore, brings countries into closer, more regular touch with those other members with whom they would not otherwise have much in common, and so extends their range of diplomatic experience and contact.

This very range of geography and alignments, of which apologists for the Commonwealth like to boast, also means that it can virtually never act as a unit on any matter of substance. Aid may be channeled from its richer to its poorer members, but the Commonwealth is not an economic entity. It could never be a military alliance or even a diplomatic unit. At a diplomatic level, it is little more than an arrangement for consultation and discussion. As such it may be extremely useful and amounts to much more than the periodic conferences of Commonwealth prime ministers. There is a regular flow of information among Commonwealth governments and among their representatives at most international organizations, including the United Nations.

Inevitably, however, on many important matters, other relationships take precedence. For most members, regional trade and political relations have become paramount. For Australia and New Zealand—especially the latter—the relationships with other countries of southern and eastern Asia have progressively come to matter more. For the African members, there are the Organization of African Unity and the United Nations. For Britain, there are NATO and Europe.

There have also been social changes. The pattern of immigration into Australia, for example, has brought in many people who are not of British origin and who do not have the same emotional links with the mother country. This has led to the development of an Australian identity that is distinct from the Australian relationship with the United Kingdom.

There have been parallel developments in Canada as well. The increasing tension between French Canada and the rest of Canada —which does not mean just Canadians of British origin, since there has been a large influx of other immigrants, especially from central Europe, during the postwar years—has made it necessary to emphasize the Canadian national identity as distinct again from the Canadian relationship with Britain, or with France, or with the United States for that matter. Thus, Canada decided in the 1960s to have a new flag and a new national anthem of its own. Canada has also sought its own diplomatic role in the world. It has remained a loyal and active member of the Commonwealth; but membership has been suspect in French Canada, and regarded as too much an indication of the British connection, for it to be the principal focus of Canadian international activity. This explains why Canada has been so enthusiastic a member of the United Nations: there Canada can play a constructive role without seeming to give priority to any links with Britain, France, or the United States.

The Commonwealth has also lost favor in British eyes because time and again, especially at prime ministers' conferences, it came to be seen above all as an organization that applied pressure on Britain to pursue policies that Britain would not otherwise have pursued. This pressure was most evident in the case of Rhodesia. Whatever the rights and wrongs of the Rhodesian policy of successive British governments—and nobody could pretend that it has been throughout a success story—Britain was belabored at a number of prime ministers' conferences in the 1960s and early 1970s for its failure to achieve what it was then probably incapable of achieving—namely, reassertion of British authority in Rhodesia and direction of the course of events there.

Southern Rhodesia had become a self-governing colony within the British Empire as long ago as 1923. From then on it was to all intents and purposes run by the white settler community, with a governor appointed by the Crown. In 1953 the Central African Federation was formed of Southern Rhodesia together with the colonies of Northern Rhodesia and Nyasaland—now respectively, Zambia and Malawi, independent states within the Commonwealth. The motive for this federation was largely economic: with Southern Rhodesia joined to the copper belt of Northern Rhodesia, it was believed that the new federation would be an economically viable state. There was also the hope that this might develop into a genuine multiracial nation in the heart of Africa: the much smaller proportion of white settlers in Northern Rhodesia and Nyasaland had never assumed political control in those countries, which remained colonies under the government of the British Colonial Office. The dream of a multiracial haven was never realized. The black majorities of Northern Rhodesia and Nyasaland were never reconciled to the federation, which had not been granted the status of an independent state and was dissolved by the British government in 1963.

Having failed to become independent as part of the federation, Southern Rhodesia—or plain Rhodesia, as it became known after Northern Rhodesia was given its independence as Zambia in 1964 —sought to become independent in its own right. Independence was refused by successive British governments unless certain conditions, known as the "six principles," were fulfilled. The most important of these were that the constitution should provide for unimpeded progress toward majority rule, and that independence should be approved by the majority of the Rhodesian people, who were black. The two conditions were obviously linked; and neither was likely to be met at a time when one of the principal purposes of the Rhodesian demand for independence was to ensure that the white community would have the authority to continue running the country.

Although the British government was able to withhold consent to Rhodesia's being given independence constitutionally, it could

not prevent Rhodesia from seizing independence for itself. The Unilateral Declaration of Independence (UDI), which was made in November 1965 by Ian Smith, the Prime Minister of Rhodesia, turned the administration of that country into an illegal regime. It was a rebel government not recognized in international law because it was in revolt against the constitutional authority—the British government. The international community might nonetheless have given diplomatic recognition to the rebel regime, as it has done on countless occasions when a revolt has apparently won effective control over a country. But on this occasion, because the seizure of power by a white settler minority went against the prevailing winds of world opinion, the international community, through the United Nations, responded not by conferring diplomatic recognition but by imposing economic sanctions on the rebels.

Harold Wilson, then British Prime Minister, claimed at the Commonwealth Conference of January 1966 in Lagos that it would be a matter of "weeks rather than months" before sanctions brought the Rhodesia regime to heel. In fact, the sanction rules were ignored so widely by so many countries—including British oil companies, as later revelations were to disclose—that, although they caused Rhodesia a degree of economic hardship, it was not for another thirteen years that Mr. Smith was forced to hand over as prime minister to a black leader, Bishop Abel Muzorewa, under the terms of a new constitution. Lord Carrington's Rhodesian settlement lay even further in the future.

Although Britain had for years no effective power in Rhodesia, successive British governments found that they were repeatedly being attacked in international arenas for their policies there as if they were equally responsible in fact as in international law. Then, at the 1970 Commonwealth Conference, Britain was assailed by most other members for the declared intention of the new Heath government to sell arms to South Africa. This foolish commitment had been made by the Conservatives before they came into office, and reflected a misjudgment of the force of international, and

61

indeed of British, opinion on this matter. After insisting at the conference upon its right to sell arms, Britain subsequently sold only a few to South Africa.

The incident confirmed many British people in the judgment that in the Commonwealth Britain was always on the defensive—if not on specific, emotional issues such as these, then over the level of economic aid that Britain as the richest member gave to the developing countries of the Commonwealth.

For all these reasons—while it continues to do much valuable work, while it still has a hold upon the sentiments of a significant section of the British public, and while it has helped to cushion the psychological effects of the loss of empire—the Commonwealth has not provided for Britain a substitute for the Empire in terms of power and prestige in the world.

SUEZ AND THE MIDDLE EAST

This loss of power was brought home to the British people in devastating fashion by the Suez affair in 1956.[2] Since 1875, when Disraeli bought a majority of shares in the Suez Canal Company for the British government, the canal has been prized by all successor governments as the link from Britain to India and the East. It has also proved to be a dividing line between Britain's past and present. The trauma of 1956 was in many ways as important a dividing line as was the Second World War. As a result of the war, Britain's position in the world was immeasurably weakened. As a result of Suez, that weakness was exposed for the British people and for the rest of the world to see. In the years between Britain's power had actually declined immensely, but that decline was not quite evident. Britain tried to act at Suez as if there had been no change, and suddenly found itself in a different world.

Although the Middle East had never been part of the British

Empire, Britain had occupied Egypt militarily in 1882 and for years had dominated its government. There were British mandates for different parts of the area from both the League of Nations and the United Nations. There were the British protectorates in the Persian Gulf, where British residents or advisers were for many years largely responsible for the government of the sheikdoms. British colonial policy had indeed effectively determined the boundaries of Middle Eastern states after the First World War. So even though there has never been a British colony or dominion in the Middle East, the area has always in modern times been of great importance to the United Kingdom, first as the route to India and then because of oil. The North Africa campaigns were thus a critical part of British military operations during the Second World War.

British power and influence in the area had begun to slip before 1956. Britain's relinquishment of the Palestine mandate in 1948 had been somewhat ignominious. Britain had tried to maintain an even-handed policy between the Jews and Arabs and had satisfied nobody: it had neither recognized the state of Israel nor pleased the Arabs by giving them back their land. Various partition plans were wrangled over without success, so finally Britain simply announced that it was leaving—and thus provoked complaints that it had not fulfilled the trusteeship in decent order. The boundaries of the new state of Israel were left to be decided by the first (1948) Arab-Israel war.

In 1951, Dr. Mohammed Mosaddeq nationalized the Anglo-Iranian Oil Company's refinery at Abadan in Iran; and although he was subsequently removed from power—with the aid of the United States's Central Intelligence Agency—the episode was a disturbing disclosure to the British public of how their prosperity could be threatened by nationalist politicians in the Middle East. In 1954 another nationalist politician, Colonel Gamal Abdel Nasser, the new ruler of Egypt, had a triumph when Britain withdrew from its Canal Zone base, its last base on Egyptian territory. Then Egypt negotiated an arms deal with Czechoslovakia and so seemed to be moving under Communist influence. In the mid-1950s Glubb Pasha—General John Glubb, a British officer who had been seconded to Jordan to command the Arab Legion—was dismissed by King Hussein. And Selwyn Lloyd, the British Foreign Secretary, was harassed by a demonstration in Bahrein.

Some of these events may now seem trivial. At the time they had a cumulative effect on the British public, who took them to indicate a progressive undermining of the British position in the Middle East. Sir Anthony Eden, the British Prime Minister, was also experiencing political difficulties at home. Thus, when Nasser nationalized the Suez Canal Company in July 1956, Eden was under a double pressure to show that he could act decisively to protect British interests. There was much talk of learning the lesson of Munich, that it was essential to stand up to dictators right away. At the end of October, after months of fruitless attempts to bring effective diplomatic pressure to bear upon Nasser, Britain and France resorted to military action. There can be no doubt now that they were collaborating with Israel. When Israel launched an attack upon Egypt, the British and the French governments promptly sent the combatants an ultimatum requiring them to withdraw ten miles on either side of the canal, and announced that they would send in forces to reoccupy the Canal Zone.

The Suez venture proved disastrous from every standpoint. The novel idea of separating the combatants by seizing a strategic asset miles from the site of the fighting outraged world opinion. The venture was unsuccessful as a military operation because British and French forces were not moved to the area sufficiently quickly to prevent ships from being sunk in the canal; consequently, the canal was closed for some time. There was an alarming run on sterling. And Britain and France, under American pressure, were forced to call the whole thing off within a matter of days, leaving the way clear to a United Nations peacemaking operation.

Altogether, Suez was a humiliation that bit deep into the British national consciousness. Two principal conclusions were drawn from this disaster, and both were later to have a considerable impact on the course of British affairs. The first was that the Anglo-American alliance, the cornerstone then of British foreign policy, had its limitations. The British and French intervention had been so misconceived—morally, militarily, and politically—that the United States could not be blamed for refusing to support it; but the strength of American condemnation, both in the United Nations and in the economic pressure the United States exercised to bring the operation to an early halt, nonetheless came as a shock to British politicians and public alike. The United States was clearly not supporting its allies right or wrong or even tempering its retribution when they were in the wrong. This was all the harder a blow because American diplomatic conduct before the launching of the operation was far from blameless. The canal might never have been seized by Nasser at all if the United States, piqued by Egypt's Czechoslovakian arms deal, had not abruptly withdrawn its offer of aid for Egypt's prestige development project, the Aswan Dam—and so forced Britain to withdraw its much smaller offer, as it would not have made sense for Britain to go ahead with it alone. The United States Secretary of State, John Foster Dulles, then failed to give Britain and France the degree of cooperation he had promised in order to bring diplomatic pressure on Egypt to negotiate a settlement. It was partly in frustration at what was regarded as American duplicity that the British and the French hatched their misguided plot.

This was not the first or the last misunderstanding between Britain and the United States over the Middle East. The difficulty has generally arisen not so much from outright conflict as from a different order of priorities in interests and loyalties. Curiously enough, over Suez it was Britain and Israel who incurred American wrath for the way they acted together. For the most part, however, the American attitude to the Middle East has been conditioned by an attachment to Israel that is much stronger than Britain's. The most obvious reason for this attachment is the size of the Jewish community in the United States, which makes it sensible for any American President ultimately to be on the side of Israel. It is possible for him to disagree with Israel on important issues—as, for example, in the Carter administration's periodic irritation with Mr. Begin's government over implementation of the peace treaty with Egypt; but if any American president were seen to withdraw overall support, leaving Israel to fend entirely for itself, he would have a lot to answer for at home.

American support for Israel does not simply reflect the strength of feeling among American Jews. For many other Americans, Israel became a sentimental favorite in the postwar world in much the same way that Britain was a sentimental favorite of the United States before the Second World War.[3] There was a time in the middle and late 1930s when it would have been a plausible construction of American interests to say that the United States should be evenhanded between the global ambitions of Britain and Germany. Indeed, many prominent Americans took that view; but it was decisively rejected by most Americans, who felt that there was a fundamental sharing of cultural and political principles between Britain and the United States. For these Americans, the defeat of Britain was simply unacceptable, a threat to civilized values. Much the same sort of sentiment animates the American political position vis-à-vis Israel.

The situation is different in Britain. British statesmen played a leading role in the process that led to the creation of Israel: it was the Balfour Declaration on behalf of the British government in 1918 which first officially endorsed the principle of a Jewish national home. There is also much public sympathy in Britain for Israel as a small democratic state battling for survival. Yet the Jewish community in Britain is not so large as the one in the United States, though it is rich and not without influence.

There is also in Britain a contrary tradition that is unknown in the United States—namely, a romantic attachment to the Arabs. Only a relatively few of the British are affected by this second tradition, and it is found mostly in intellectual circles. It involves a history of semi-recreational adventuring in the Middle East, of mucking about in the Holy Land for fun and profit, of organizing against the "Huns" in the desert sands during the First World War —the kind of thing that made T. E. Lawrence, "Lawrence of Arabia," a folk hero for a time. The relationship's less dramatic side has included British expert participation in institution building in the Arab world. Thus, the tradition has included a mixture of adventure and obligation that is peculiarly appealing to a certain type of Englishman.

The tradition has helped to sustain a school of Arabist sympathizers in a section of the British foreign service, who were alleged to have influenced Ernest Bevin in 1948 when he was grappling as Foreign Secretary with the Palestine problem. There has been an American belief that the British are often soft toward the Arab states. But it would be more correct to see the British in general not as Arab sympathizers but as more aware than the Americans of conflicting interests in the Middle East. A critical factor here has been oil. For a large part of this century British prosperity has depended upon plentiful supplies of cheap oil from the Middle East; and until the North Sea oil began to flow in quantity, Britain depended upon the Middle East for a much larger proportion of its oil than did the United States.[4] This dependence certainly had a marked influence upon British diplomacy at the time of the Yom Kippur war in 1973.

Now the position has changed in two respects. The North Sea has reduced British dependence upon the Middle East, and the energy crisis has made the United States much more concerned about the price and supply of oil from there. It was not because of Israel that there was intense American anxiety over the upheaval in Iran and the Soviet action in Afghanistan. Anglo-American perspectives have grown closer, and the two countries have common interests: that such a strategically and economically sensitive area should be as stable as possible; that it should not come to be dominated by the Soviet Union; and that oil supplies should remain freely available to the international trading world.

BRITAIN'S POLITICAL AGENDA

BRITAIN AND EUROPE

The second conclusion that the British public drew from the Suez affair was that Britain, even in conjunction with France, could no longer act in defiance of the international community. Britain might still enjoy the trappings of a world power but could not afford to behave like one. This realization was a principal consideration in persuading Britain eventually—although not immediately —to join the European Economic Community. British statesmen —Winston Churchill in particular—had played a notable role in calling the European movement into being with rousing declarations of the principle of European union; but there had always been a certain fuzziness about the constitutional import of these declarations. They were expressions of a sentiment rather than a blueprint for action. Britain declined to join the European Coal and Steel Community in 1952 and the stillborn European Defense Community in 1954, and to look with favor upon the birth of the Common Market (the EEC) a few years later.

The British government had the opportunity of taking part in the Messina talks in 1955, from which the Treaty of Rome setting up the Common Market emerged in 1957, but decided not to participate, hoping and believing that nothing would come of the project. Even when that judgment proved to be mistaken, it was not until 1961 that Britain applied to join. In the meantime it had been a founder member in 1960 of the European Free Trade Area (EFTA), an organization of those European countries that had political or economic reasons for being unable to become members of the EEC.[5] EFTA had a double purpose: to work out a satisfactory relationship with the EEC, so that those outside the Community would not suffer from discrimination against them; and to encourage trade among themselves by the creation of a free trade area in industrial goods—different from the Community in that it did not have common external tariffs or supranational institutions.

68

Nor did it attempt to regulate agricultural trade. It was essentially a defensive grouping, but it was far more successful in its attempts to stimulate trade among member states than had been expected. The first formal application for Britain to join the EEC was made by Harold Macmillan as Prime Minister in August 1961.[6] There followed over a year of detailed negotiations, led on the British side by Edward Heath, then Lord Privy Seal in Mr. Macmillan's cabinet. The negotiations were difficult, because Britain was not prepared simply to accept the rules of the Community as they stood, but wanted exceptions to be made in particular so that the same level of Commonwealth exports could continue to enter Britain, and so that the existing British system of agricultural support could largely be maintained.

These detailed negotiations progressed quite well. Then, on 14 January 1963, President de Gaulle made it clear at a press conference in Paris that France would veto Britain's application. The reasons he gave, though they caused much offense in Britain then and later, in fact indicate some of the reasons that Britain had delayed before seeking to join the Community:

> England in effect is insular, she is maritime, she is linked through her exchanges, her markets, her supply lines to the most diverse and often the most distant countries; she pursues essentially industrial and commercial activities, and only slight agricultural ones. She has in all her doings very marked and very original habits and traditions. In short, the nature, the structure, the very situation that are England's differ profoundly from those of the continentals.[7]

De Gaulle was in effect endorsing Churchill's earlier dictum that if Britain ever had to choose between Europe and the open sea, it would choose the open sea. It would be a mistake to conclude that Britain was held back from Europe principally by the Commonwealth connection. This consideration certainly had a strong hold on a section of British opinion, which believed that Britain could not for long be the center of a thriving Commonwealth and a member of the European Community. Britain had traditionally bought much of its food cheaply from the Commonwealth, and there were some anxieties over the economic implications of more expensive food, which was believed would result from accepting the EEC's Common Agricultural Policy. And political embarrassment was created by the leaders of some Commonwealth governments—most notably by John Diefenbaker, the Canadian Prime Minister, at the Commonwealth Conference in September 1962—after Mr. Macmillan had made his application.

Commonwealth trade was, however, no longer so important to Britain as it had been. Whereas in 1956, 46 percent of British exports had gone to the Commonwealth, that figure was down to 36.0 percent in 1960 and was to fall still farther, to 24 percent, by the time of Britain's second abortive attempt to join the Community in 1967. Nor was there much prospect of this trend being reversed, as the industrial economies of Western Europe were expanding much faster. Moreover, by the early 1960s the weaknesses of the Commonwealth as a diplomatic association were already apparent. So far as British entry to the EEC was concerned, the Commonwealth was an embarrassment not a blockage.

When de Gaulle spoke of Britain's maritime links, he was not referring only to the Commonwealth. If Britain and other members of EFTA were to join, the Community "would be faced with the problems of its economic relations with all sorts of other nations, and first of all with the United States. It is to be foreseen that the cohesion of its members, who would be very numerous and diverse, would not endure for long, and that finally it would appear as a colossal Atlantic community under American domination and direction which would quickly have absorbed the European Community." This fear of de Gaulle's that the British would be America's Trojan horse was the single most important reason for his veto. In December 1962, just before his veto, he had been visited by Mr. Macmillan at Rambouillet. Macmillan believed then that he had obtained de Gaulle's agreement to British membership, and immediately after he flew to Nassau for a meeting with U.S. President John F. Kennedy.

At this time Kennedy told Macmillan of the cancellation of the Skybolt missile on which Britain's future plans for its nuclear force were based, and, after much argument, it was agreed that Britain should have the Polaris missile fitted to British submarines.[8] This episode symbolized for de Gaulle the acceptance by Britain of an unbreakable tie with the United States: the Americans were cancelling Skybolt without regard for their ally, and Britain was then tamely accepting the next offer they put forward. The issue was in fact more complex, but it seemed to the French that the British were compromising the independence of their nuclear force and becoming American stooges.

The British naturally did not see themselves in this light. It was true, however, that they did prize the Atlantic relationship as a cornerstone of British foreign policy. The Anglo-American partnership had provided the basis for victory in the Second World War. The international monetary system devised in 1944 at Bretton Woods in New Hampshire was founded on the strength of the dollar; and the United States was the heart and core of the North Atlantic Treaty Organization. The key issues of military and economic security seemed to depend above all on the United States; and it was the fear of weakening this connection—for the sake of joining a European Community that showed no signs of developing a sufficient defense capacity of its own and was not by itself able to secure international monetary stability—that was principally responsible for Britain's European hesitations. There was much talk in those years of building up Europe in order to strengthen the broader Atlantic community; but when de Gaulle made it clear that he viewed an Atlantic community as a threat, confirmed Atlanticists became all the more uneasy about the EEC. Churchill and Eden had often spoken of basing British foreign policy upon three interlocking circles—the links with Europe, the Commonwealth, and the United States. Many British people were worried that, in order to qualify for membership in the European Community, they seemed to be required to cast aside the other two circles. And there were all the fears that the supranational institutions of the Community would interfere with traditional British sovereignty. Where would the process of integration stop? Would it be compatible in the long run with keeping the monarchy? It is not for nothing that the British are known as a conservative people.

Yet it was not because of these uncertainties, but because of de Gaulle's veto, that Britain did not join in 1963 or again in 1967 when Harold Wilson, by then Prime Minister, and his Foreign Secretary, George Brown, toured the six capitals of the EEC countries in the hope of winning acceptance of British membership. Only in 1973, after de Gaulle's death, did Britain finally join. Why were successive British governments so persistent after such initial reluctance? It was certainly not because of popular pressure. The British have always had their suspicions about the continent of Europe. There is where they have had to go to fight wars. The British are bad linguists and parochial in their attitudes. If a referendum had been held before Britain joined, it is doubtful if there would ever have been a majority for membership. It is true that in 1975, after the incoming Labour government had marginally renegotiated the terms of entry, there was a referendum majority of nearly two to one in favor of Britain remaining in the Community; but by then the advocates of membership were able to base their case on caution and the status quo.

The EEC cause has to some extent always been an élitist one in Britain. It was leaders in government, in the Civil Service, in industry and the professions, who became convinced that membership was necessary. They were persuaded by a number of considerations. One was economic. Western Europe was expanding fast, much faster than the Commonwealth; and there was the prospect of being part of an entity with a combined home market of two hundred million people—compared with a mere fifty-five million in Britain. It was also felt that British industry would benefit from the bracing effects of competition, just as Britain had been the economic leader of the Western world in the nineteenth century when it had practiced the doctrine of free trade.

Then there was the desire to have a greater impact on world

events. Britain was no longer a superpower, but the leaders of the principal institutions in Britain still retained the instincts of people accustomed to running one. That was the style in which they had been brought up. The British public in general, although not themselves accustomed to exercising such power, had always assumed that they lived in a country that could play a major part in determining the course of history. British patriotism was based on a sense of historical pride, not just on an attachment to home. It had been a shock at the time of the Suez affair to find that their country's power was diminished. In that respect, entry to the Community could be regarded as a delayed reaction to Suez. As Dean Acheson, the former American Secretary of State, said in December 1962, just before the first de Gaulle veto, Britain had "lost an empire and had not yet found a role."[9] In looking to Europe, Britain was seeking to find one.

The British were all the more inclined to look in that direction because on closer examination the Anglo-American alternative did not seem to exist. It is impossible to have a particularly close relationship with another country when the other country does not want the bilateral relationship to be equally close. As the United States saw it, a bilateral Atlantic alliance was no longer a practical alternative, because the British link was too weak by itself and needed to be bolstered by association with the rest of Western Europe. Britain was forced to conclude that the United States was prepared to live in a commune with her, but not to marry her.

American pressure on British leaders to join the Community was important in a positive as well as a negative fashion. It encouraged British leaders to believe that joining would contribute to the general strength of the West. In July 1962, President Kennedy delivered an address which attracted much attention and in which he stressed that the Atlantic Community rested upon twin pillars. Americans saw the British task as being to strengthen the European pillar. American strategic planners had always liked the idea of a united Europe, which they saw as a bulwark against the westward spread of communism. There are some weak links in the

Western alliance, and it was widely believed that they could more efficiently be sustained economically and politically by bringing them into a European economic system. This arrangement seemed to American strategists to be a logical successor to the Marshall Plan and the Point Four program of the era immediately following the Second World War.

The role of Britain in such an enterprise was potentially significant. In Britain there is no domestic threat of communism. Britain has a history of political stability, and in those days at any rate it was credited with political accomplishments of a high order. Britain was also seen in the United States as capable of taking a global view and bringing worldwide perspectives to the councils of the European Community, which seemed to Americans to be highly desirable for a strengthened and more interdependent Europe. There is always the danger, as Americans see it, of Franco-German rivalry dominating West European politics, and of the French becoming excessively parochial. The presence of Britain was thought to be the best counter to both these risks.[10]

British experience within the Community can be judged on two levels. One is on the plane of practical policies. How easily has Britain adapted to the EEC? It is probably inevitable in any political system that grievances attract the most attention; and that has certainly been the case in this instance. On the British side there has been a general grumble and a series of specific complaints. In general terms, British people have tended to feel that the Community interferes, indeed fusses, too much on points of small detail. An amusing article on this theme by Ferdinand Mount, political correspondent of the British magazine the *Spectator,* began with a reference to an EEC Commission proposal for a Community directive entitled "Less Noisy Lawn Mowers."[11] Then there was the saga of the tachograph, the "spy in the cab." The tachograph is an instrument for measuring a journey's length, time, and speed; and its installation in all commercial trucks throughout the Community as a means of securing uniform compliance with EEC regulations was strenuously resisted by British lorry drivers. The urge to harmonize conditions throughout the Community has led to its being associated in many British minds with the over-regulation and over-government that are so unpopular in the Western world these days.

The specific complaints of substance are a greater source of resentment. The Common Agricultural Policy (CAP) is intensely unpopular because it is associated in British minds with over-production and high prices. Britain, as de Gaulle pointed out, has a relatively small agricultural sector—and, it should be added, a much more efficient one than France has;[12] and its principal interest is therefore to protect the consumer rather than to cosset the farmer. So the high guaranteed prices of the CAP, which have led to over-production in some commodities—creating butter mountains and wine lakes, some of which have had to be sold off to the Soviet consumer at knockdown prices—have been a particular affront to the British as an obviously unnecessary subsidy of the farmer. The CAP has also pushed up prices for the British housewife. John Kay, the research director of the highly respected Institute for Fiscal Studies, has calculated that following the increase of 5 percent in farm prices agreed by the Community in May 1980, British housewives would in the future pay about three thousand million pounds more for food a year through the Common Agricultural Policy than they would if the United Kingdom were able to buy on the cheaper world markets—as it used to do before joining the EEC.[13]

The CAP is undoubtedly a wasteful system. This was the main reason that the issue of Britain's net contribution to the Community budget became so acute. The CAP accounts for about three quarters of that budget; and Britain, with its small agricultural sector, derives relatively little from it. Also, the system of levies on imports into the Community penalizes those countries with a high ratio of trade outside the Community, and Britain has more trade outside the Community than any other member. So Britain was suffering on both sides of the ledger, in terms of high payments into the Community budget and low receipts from it; so that although it has the third lowest standard of living of any member, it was becoming the largest net contributor.

It was in order to rectify this inequity, as it seemed to British eyes, that Mrs. Thatcher embarked on a series of bitter negotiations with other heads of government in the Community during 1979 and early 1980. The matter was finally settled by a compromise agreement at a meeting of Community foreign ministers in Brussels at the end of May 1980.

This did not resolve all issues between Britain and the rest of the Community, but particular grievances, especially in the early years of an association, really matter only insofar as they feed a more general discontent. This brings us to the second, and much more important, level at which British experience within the EEC is to be judged. How far has it provided the British with a new sphere of operation, as distinct from purely technical advantages or handicaps? How far are they coming to feel that they are both British and European, in the same way that the Scots in an earlier age came to accept that they were both Scottish and British?

Of all the countries that negotiated to join the Community in 1973, only the United Kingdom did not put the decision to a referendum. The Danes and the Irish electorates approved membership; the Norwegians rejected it, and their government abided by that decision. The British referendum did not come until 1975. The Labour party had decided, in order not to split apart over the EEC while in opposition, that when they were returned to office they would try to renegotiate the terms of British entry and then seek the guidance of the electorate. After Labour took over the government in February 1974, this process was set in motion. The actual renegotiation was largely a farce. Among the more important matters supposedly renegotiated were the CAP and the Community budget, which remained prime causes of dissatisfaction. The Cabinet agreed to differ over recommending that the country should stay in the EEC on the basis of the renegotiated terms, with a majority in favor—as were both the Conservative and the Liberal parties. So, too, was the electorate, voting for membership by 67.2

percent to 32.8 percent—with favorable majorities in England, Scotland, Wales, and Northern Ireland.

This vote should have settled the question once and for all, but it has not quite done so. Whether British membership itself will again be at issue is likely to depend partly on how the Community develops, and partly on what happens within the Labour party. Indeed, the party suggested, in its official manifesto for the European parliamentary elections in June 1979, that Britain should withdraw if certain improvements to the Community were not made.

It is much more probable that the United Kingdom will remain a member, though public opinion at home will force every successive British government to fight strongly for British interests at Brussels. How far, though, can Britain—as an awkward, not fully committed member—achieve the full benefits that were anticipated? Obviously, unless a sense of European identity develops, Europe cannot begin to act as a superpower. That sense does not yet exist. Europe today is still a collection of countries which, by pooling their strength, have certainly increased it internationally; but the EEC has not so far provided Britain with the new power base, the fresh sense of international purpose, for which the nation was looking.

Such a judgment must, however, be set in perspective. First, the perspective of time. It would be foolish when Britain has been a member of the Community for less than a decade to settle on a long-term judgment. Second, there is the perspective of economic circumstances. The century after the Union of the Parliaments between England and Scotland was a time of prosperity, as were the first years of the Common Market before Britain joined. This naturally made people attribute their blessings partly to constitutional change, whether this was a cause or a coincidence. Conversely, in the economic gloom that has obtained since Britain joined the EEC, it is not surprising that people have been looking for a scapegoat. On the assumption that Europe will enjoy prosperity again before the end of this century, it makes sense to wait and see how a touch of the sun changes the British view of the Community. Finally, there is the perspective of political conditions. Only with the first direct elections to the European Parliament in June 1979 are Community-wide political groupings beginning to develop. The Parliament itself has as yet only limited powers, and the campaign and election in Britain did not betray signs of much recognition or enthusiasm for it: the turn-out of 33 percent was by far the lowest of all member countries. The key question is whether over the years there will develop a genuinely European political scene, with European parties competing and collaborating on European issues. Such a development will measure how far the Community plays a part in the lives of the British people as well as in the British government—though one should note how already the decisions emanating from Brussels are quietly and steadily bringing law and practice into line among the different member countries.

ANGLO-AMERICAN RELATIONS

Although Britain went into the EEC with the full encouragement of the United States, the European connection did complicate Anglo-American relations. It was because Britain was thought to be too close to the United States that the former was kept out of the Community on the first two occasions that it tried to join. Therefore there was a tendency among the most pro-European of the British to demonstrate, by exaggerating the distance between Britain and America, to potential partners in Europe that Britain was fit to join them. They did not become so much anti-American as rather cool toward America. In a reversal of the historic roles between the two countries, it was almost like a restive teen-ager seeking to assert a separate identity from its parents.

The growing disparity in military and economic strength between the two countries also weakened the relationship. We have mentioned that this was one of the reasons that the United States wanted Britain in Europe. Perhaps inevitably, the British appreciation that a bilateral relationship was not sufficient for America developed into a somewhat sour belief that no bilateral relationship at all was still possible. A fruitless debate has been conducted in Britain during the postwar years—characterized by sentimentalism on the one side and by excessive self-denigration on the other —over whether the "special relationship" was dead. The British mood swung from exaggerating the United Kingdom's importance to America to underestimating that importance.

In fact, the tie with the United States is sentimental and close. This is something that exists irrespective of the wishes of politicians or the drift of public policy on either side. There are the bonds of history, of language, of the common law tradition, and of the practice of democratic politics for a longer continuous period than in nearly any other country. It has become fashionable to point out that the apparent similarities in customs and institutions conceal a wealth of differences. This insight is true, provided that too much is not made of the differences. British and Americans do find it easier to understand each other—and even, with a minimum of effort, each other's politics—than do the people of most other countries. This understanding is not altogether surprising. There are nearly half as many people in the United States of British ancestry as there are in Britain: twenty-six million in the United States compared with fifty-five million in the United Kingdom. Likewise there are four times as many people of Irish ancestry in the United States as there are in Ireland.[14] Virtually every President of the United States has been able to trace at least one ancestor to the British Isles, and the vast preponderance of American Presidents could trace all their ancestors there.

Such connections, important though they are, do not guarantee that one country will look favorably upon another. The way in which the United States is regarded in Britain varies enormously, partly according to how America actually conducts its policies at any given moment, and partly according to the style of its leader. It is hardly surprising that Vietnam and Watergate damaged the United States nearly as much in British eyes as they did in American eyes. President Carter's initial emphasis upon human rights issues in foreign policy did much to reconcile British left-wing opinion, which during the postwar years has been far more inclined to be hostile to the United States. In other quarters, Mr. Carter's stand was taken as evidence of naïveté.

An American president who has the capacity to project his personality and his ideas beyond the shores of the United States can receive an enormous welcome in Britain and be regarded almost as a leader of the British people. He can make the Atlantic Community seem a reality. One of the misfortunes both for the United States and for its closest allies is that no American president since John Kennedy has been able to project his personality in this way. The British felt an identification with Kennedy, with Eisenhower, and to a lesser extent with Truman. Roosevelt was a very great figure in Britain during the war years. Although he was never president, Adlai Stevenson also performed an immense service for America in contributing to the way the United States was perceived in Britain. During the McCarthy years, when the political stories emanating from the United States were mostly of prejudice, persecution, and pusillanimity, he seemed to represent an assurance of the continuing decency of American public life—an assurance that has been needed on occasion since then.

Despite the ups and downs of recent years, the conditions for a close Anglo-American relationship remain. So does the need for it. Particularly after Vietnam, the United States feels more comfortable when acting in Africa, the Middle East, or in Asia if it does so with the active cooperation of its European allies, and especially of the United Kingdom.

The relationship is also of critical importance to Britain nearer home. A middle-sized power has a greater interest in alliance than a superpower has. A superpower often depends more on its alliances than it realizes, particularly for psychological and political reasons; but for a middle-sized power, alliances are of overriding importance for military reasons. NATO matters at one level in terms of the members deploying their strength on the ground in Europe to prevent any exercise of Soviet military power that would present the alliance with a *fait accompli.* A much greater interest of the middle-sized European powers of the West is to preserve the American nuclear commitment to all of the alliance, and to ensure that this commitment remains not only strong but credible. It is for this reason that Britain, and America's other European allies, attach so much importance to the stationing of American troops in Europe. What matters is not that there should be a particular number of American troops on European soil, but that the commitment of troops should be of a sufficient size as to make it inevitable that the United States would immediately become directly involved in defending any of its European allies that was attacked.

It is this consideration that makes the contrast between Britain's European and American attachments a logical absurdity. So long as Western Europe does not itself possess the military power, nuclear and conventional, capable of checking the Soviet Union, every European member of NATO has a direct military, political, and psychological interest in keeping warm the American relationship. For Britain, as a middle-sized power dependent on its alliances, it is those with Europe and the United States that matter above all others these days.

Even if Britain gets its priorities and relationships right, how much impact can it really have in the contemporary world? It is interesting that within the last sixteen years there have been three major reviews of Britain's diplomatic service, and two of them have concluded that it is overextended. The Plowden Report of 1964, reflecting the attitudes of more assured days, recommended no more than technical or detailed adjustments.[15] The Duncan report of 1969 went much farther.[16] It proposed that, for the purposes of diplomatic representation, the world should be divided into two groups: one, the Area of Concentration, would comprise about a dozen countries in Western Europe and North America, plus a few others like Australia and Japan, with whom Britain's relations would be very important. In this area Britain's diplomatic commitment would be heavy. Elsewhere it could be reduced, though there was no suggestion of eliminating it. Then in 1977 the Central Policy Review Staff (CPRS)—the "Cabinet's think tank," as it is known—produced the most radical report of the lot.[17] It is not necessary to summarize all its many recommendations, except to indicate that the report was based on the propositions that, for a country in Britain's position, economic activity and export promotion were the first priorities, and that the scale of the diplomatic operation altogether should be reduced.

The main theme of the Duncan report was not adopted, and the CPRS report was badly received.[18] Their precise recommendations are therefore of less consequence than the assumptions on which they were based, especially the assumptions of the CPRS report. Its authors clearly believe that Britain no longer has the power to conduct much of a foreign policy in the traditional sense. It is a measure of Britain's decline that this judgment should infuse an official report of this nature; but it is still more a measure of the fall in confidence that has accompanied this decline.

Just as Britain exaggerated its strength in the decade from the end of the war until Suez, so now Britain may fail to appreciate the influence it retains. A middle-sized power like Britain —especially one with its links to the United States, its membership in the EEC, and its Commonwealth connections—is well placed to play a useful role in many parts of the world. It is a role based upon its experience, its diplomatic skills—which are more highly regarded in many other countries than British opinion recognizes—and its capacity to offer good advice. For those purposes Britain's inability to wield the same power as of old is of little consequence. Britain has become so obsessed by its economic difficulties that it is in danger of asking its diplomats to forsake the conduct of diplomatic and political relations, for which they are well trained, for the sake of performing as export salesmen, for which they are ill equipped. An increase of effort on the one front need not be accompanied by the phasing-out of the other. And Britain will never perform any role usefully unless it recovers the confidence to do so.

PART II

POLITICAL MACHINERY AND THE
PROMOTION OF DEMOCRATIC
VALUES: PARTIES, PARLIAMENT
AND GOVERNMENT, PUBLIC
ADMINISTRATION

The instruments available in the United Kingdom to deal with political problems are venerable and venerated—the product of centuries of evolution and quite a lot of tinkering. How well Britain is able to manage, in the end, will largely be determined by the flexibility and the intelligence with which these instruments are used. Thus our discussion of political machinery focuses upon issues of flexibility and responsiveness, and upon the maintenance and enhancement of democratic values in the face of the severe national problems we have been discussing. Parties are instruments for defining issues and mobilizing public support, but for government to be effective, a degree of consensus about policy is necessary. We therefore look at the relation between Parliament and government in light of the need to enlist a broad range of participation and consent for policy to have its desired effects. Finally, we examine the administration of public policy and the Civil Service with attention to the strong and varied contemporary pressures to incorporate greater professionalism and to promote enlightened public discussion of policy before it is settled upon as a prerequisite to its successful implementation.

CHAPTER 4

Political Parties and the Management of Social Consensus

A key contemporary question for British politics, as it is for the politics of any democratic nation, is whether it is possible to fashion a consensus adequate to allow successive governments, possibly of different parties, to run the country. This question is relevant even in the light of the strong Conservative victory in the 1979 parliamentary election. Because, regardless of electoral majorities and of the constitutional privileges that go with the capacity to organize a government in Parliament, the consent to govern in any complex modern society rests not only upon the verdict of the electorate every few years, but also upon acceptance by many and varied institutions. One of the most important instruments for obtaining this acceptance as well as for winning elections is the political party. Consensus, however, does not entail the elimination of conflict and competition between the parties. That would be quite impossible under the British system. And, indeed, it would not be desirable.

British parliamentary government is based upon parties to a degree that is unknown in the United States. American politics is fragmented in the sense that much of it consists of competition among leading political figures—party leaders, public officials, and presidential candidates—with their own retainers and their own local armies. A Jimmy Carter can come from nowhere to the presidency of the United States because party organization is loose and ineffective, and one who is a serious candidate needs to build an organization of his own to have a chance of winning the nomination of his party and then the presidential election itself. In order to begin this process, one need not be the choice of party elders. It is of little consequence before the election whether one is a congressional favorite. If one has enough popular appeal, one can climb to power regardless of regular party organizations.

In Britain, it is quite different: a person can become prime minister only after his or her party wins enough seats in the House of Commons to form a government. The leader of the party with the most seats, selected by the party's members of Parliament, then ordinarily becomes prime minister. The personality of a party leader is electorally important, but not important enough to prevent the Conservatives from winning in 1979 when Margaret Thatcher was consistently less popular than James Callaghan in the opinion polls. In 1970, Edward Heath was also less popular than Harold Wilson: yet the Conservatives won then as well. Indeed, a party can be penalized in Britain if it seems to be relying too heavily on the personal appeal of its leader—which is one of the reasons that the Labour party under Clement Attlee was able to trounce the Conservatives in 1945 when Winston Churchill was at the height of his fame.

British political parties can best be compared to a large corporation, in which one scrambles up the greasy pole until one wins a seat on the board. In this progress what matters is the opinion of one's peers and superiors within the organization. Outsiders may bestow praise or criticism, but they cannot give or withhold promotion. The aspiring politician will be chosen, by local party activists, from a centrally approved roster to fight in a particular constituency. Unless it is a marginal seat, one's party label will determine whether one wins it.[1] If the seat is safe for one's party, whether Labour or Conservative, one can expect to go on holding it so long as one retains the confidence of the local party leaders, without worrying about one's personal standing with the general public. But only if the party is successful overall can the politician secure the rewards of success: not merely a seat in Parliament but also the chance to participate in running the government.

The fact that party competition is all-important often leads to what is regarded as the excessively adversarial nature of British politics.[2] In some countries the public expects the parties to agree wherever they can. Thus, in West Germany and Scandinavia there is popular disapproval of parties that are thought to be unnecessarily fractious. In the United States there is often a wide measure of agreement on policies across parties—as well as disagreement within them; and cross-party coalitions in Congress are common. In Britain the pressures of the parliamentary system magnify the disagreement between parties. There is a tradition that it is the duty of the opposition to oppose. Whereas the tone of American politics may often strike a British observer as boringly bland, British politics seems to overseas observers to be conducted in the spirit of a perpetual cat fight. There is more political extremism within the major parties in Great Britain than Americans are accustomed to seeing, from virtual communists on the Labour left to racist, nationalist reactionaries on the Tory right.[3]

POSTWAR CONSENSUS

Yet, despite all appearances, there is often considerable underlying agreement which may determine general assumptions across party boundaries about what the government of the day ought to be doing. Some of the most successful periods of government are those when this agreement is greatest. Typically, these are periods in which moderates control both major parties. There were, for example, the so-called Butskellite years of the 1950s, which are now looked back upon as a period of content and ordered progress.[4]

For most of the present century it has been assumed that the Conservatives are the natural governing party, with interludes of Liberal and Labour rule. But the government that did more than any other to determine the conduct of affairs throughout the postwar years was Clement Attlee's Labour administration of 1945–51, which nationalized most of Britain's basic industries and services. Electricity, gas, coal, steel, and the railways, for example, were brought under the ownership of large public corporations. The Attlee government determined the basic structure of the welfare state, creating the National Health Service and a comprehensive system of social insurance.

The Attlee government established another precedent, less tangible but in the long run no less important—belief in an activist government. To some extent this was a natural sequel to the experience of war, when the Churchill coalition government had mobilized all the resources of the country in the struggle against Hitler. A degree of government direction of the nation's activities, which would otherwise have been deeply resented, was accepted happily enough in those perilous conditions. Even rationing of food, clothes, and other necessities was a subject of humor rather than of protest. The country became acclimatized to a policy of interventionism. It was understandable then that people asked why, if government intervention was so successful in winning the war, would it not be equally effective in solving the problems of peace? The Churchill coalition prepared much of the ground for the policies with which the Attlee government is particularly associated.

The railways were brought under effective government control during wartime. The Beveridge Report on social security—which formed the basis of the Labour program, though it was not followed in every particular—was published in 1943, while the war was still at its height, and was accepted in principle by the bipartisan Churchill coalition after some initial hesitations. The coalition also had a plan for a national health service, though this was not the precise scheme that was later implemented by Labour. And the 1944 White Paper with its commitment to full employment was also the work of the coalition.

The development of the belief in an activist government was also a reaction against the suffering of the economic depression between the world wars. To describe the governments of those days as passive in the midst of catastrophe would be unfair. They were not simple apostles of the doctrine of laissez-faire or oblivious to the economic and social disaster around them. But one of the most powerful public sentiments at the end of the war was that the return to peace must not mean a return to those days of distress.

The Attlee administration's belief in the efficacy of government intervention was based on Labour's own collectivist principles, the tradition of Fabian socialism together with the development of Keynesian economics. This last appeared to provide a government with the necessary instruments for the management of the economy. Interventionism was acceptable to the public at large because there were certain things that they wanted the government to provide. They wanted a service to give health care irrespective of the individual's capacity to pay. They wanted a social security system to eliminate gross poverty in old age, sickness, and unemployment. They wanted the government to secure conditions of economic prosperity. It was but a short step from there to expect the government to deal with all emergencies and then with all problems. The desire for specific intervention led to an expectation of general intervention. "What is the government going to do about it?" became the natural question to ask whenever things went wrong. In Britain's circumstances over the past twenty years there have been plenty of occasions to put that question.

The structures and assumptions developed by the Attlee government have been adjusted and modified by succeeding administrations—but not seriously challenged until recently. After the defeat of Attlee in 1951, Churchill came back to power, this time leading a purely Conservative government. Churchill had campaigned in opposition on the theme of "set the people free," and his administration did indeed sweep away many of the remaining wartime regulations and restrictions. Rationing was finally abolished. There was less detailed intervention in the running of the economy, and more emphasis on personal incentives and on monetary controls.

Churchill also wanted, however, to demonstrate that the Conservatives—who had been in office either by themselves or as the dominant partner in a coalition for most of the years between the wars, and who were held particularly responsible for the miseries of the Depression—could govern moderately and acceptably. As Minister of Labour he appointed a man of notably conciliatory temperament, Walter Monckton, to show that the Conservatives could get along with the unions. The framework of the welfare state was left essentially unchanged. The nationalization of the basic industries was accepted as a *fait accompli,* with the exception of steel and road haulage. No less important, the concept of an activist government was accepted as well. It is significant that Harold Macmillan—a reformist Tory—established his political reputation as the minister responsible for fulfilling the Conservative election pledge to see that 300,000 houses were built a year—a total never reached under Labour.

Churchill's second premiership from 1951 to 1955 was the beginning of thirteen continuous years of Conservative rule. The dominant figure in the second half of that period was Harold Macmillan, who was Prime Minister from the beginning of 1957—when he succeeded Anthony Eden immediately after the Suez fiasco—until 1963. Macmillan's political outlook had been fashioned during the interwar years as M.P. for Stockton in the northeast of England where unemployment had been especially severe. Macmillan was left with a lasting horror of the miseries of unemployment and with a deep belief in the need for governments to act so as to prevent a recurrence of those days. He was consequently reluctant to restrict public expenditure too much and eager to pursue constructive governmental policies to secure economic prosperity. It was at his personal instigation that the first steps were taken down the interventionist path toward a managed incomes policy. He also favored more general planning of the economy and established the National Economic Development Council (Neddy), on which government, trade unions, and employers are represented. So, for one reason and another, what came to be known as the moderate forces of Conservatism—wary of the unmodified operation of the free market and close to the center of British politics—were firmly in control during those long years of the party's dominance.

Well before the Conservatives were defeated in 1964, it could reasonably be maintained that a new consensus had been established in British politics including the majority of members of both major parties, most party leaders, and most of the general public. The main elements of this consensus, which were rarely deliberately articulated but which arose from the experience of successive Labour and Conservative governments, included an extensive system of social welfare—though the British complacently went on believing that theirs was the best in the world long after it had been overtaken by a good many European countries; heavy taxation to pay for welfare; considerable government intervention in the economic, industrial, environmental, and social fields; respect amounting often to deference toward the trade unions; a relatively large public sector of industry but no eagerness to have either much more or much less nationalization. The industries that were nationalized were for the most part those that had had difficulties in private ownership, so it was not altogether surprising that the mere act of bringing them into public ownership did not give them the commercial kiss of life. Nationalized industries became associated in the public mind with unsuccessful industries forever in the red. There was more to the criticism of nationalization than this. The form of nationalization preferred was the large public corporation always associated with the name of its leading advocate, Herbert Morrison.[5] Usually covering a whole industry, and largely insulated from the pressure of market forces, large public corporations generally proved to be unwieldy, impersonal, and far less responsive to the wishes of consumers than to those of their own, heavily organized, labor force. Nor could it be maintained that those working in nationalized industries were inspired by a new élan and spirit of service, as the more ardent advocates of public ownership had hoped. The charge that nationalized industries were inefficient as well as unprofitable rested upon more substantial grounds than political malice.

Nationalization soon became a dirty word with the general public. Yet while the Conservatives relished the political advantage and made the most of it in their propaganda, branding Labour as the party of nationalization, they did not propose to denationalize most of what had already been taken into public ownership. Rather, they tacitly accepted the deed while reviling those responsible for it. Labour, on the other hand, while defending the principle and so far as possible the practice of nationalization, nonetheless went slow on the idea of bringing additional industries into public ownership. From their different doctrinal standpoints, and behind smokescreens of contrasting rhetoric, both parties largely accepted the status quo.

The thirteen years of Conservative rule were followed by the first Wilson era, from 1964 to 1970. It was Harold Wilson's ambition as Prime Minister to turn Labour into the natural governing party of the nation. So it was logical for him to proceed along the broad lines of the consensus that already existed. There was much talk of the marriage of science and socialism, the theme of Wilson's address in 1963 at the last party conference before his election victory. What this theme seemed to imply was the pursuit by more efficient means of widely accepted goals. These were years not of ideological reform but of pragmatic and often desperate measures to stave off one economic crisis after another.

To some extent economic difficulties forced pragmatism upon the Wilson government. Any administration that is trying to free itself from economic quicksand is likely to turn in whatever direction that it may discern firm ground, without much regard for preconceived ideas. There was more, however, to Wilsonian pragmatism. A party that aspires to be the natural governing party cannot afford to be consistently ideological. It is not only that most of the time the bulk of the British voting public are somewhat skeptical of ideologies; but even if they had a greater taste for political doctrine than is true of any mass public known to social science, it would be hard to find a precisely defined set of principles that would accord with their wishes at all times and under all circumstances.[6] In order to be the party to which the country naturally turns as a matter of course, it is necessary to be somewhat fuzzy at the edges—to what its friends would describe as immensely flexible and its critics would term being all things to all men.

It is no coincidence that when the Conservatives were indisputably the natural governing party—especially between the world wars after the break-up of the Liberals and before the postwar rise of Labour—they gloried in their freedom from the tyranny of doctrine. They have been derided by their opponents, and by intellectuals as far back as John Stuart Mill, as the stupid party; but they have been shrewd enough to be able to win the favor of the electorate over considerable periods of time. They have traditionally seen themselves as the party of balance, as preventing the country from lurching too far in any direction. The task of Conservatives was to correct any tendency toward extreme laissez-faire as well as toward state control. Their boast was that they would safeguard the nation against taking any doctrine of the day too far.

Harold Wilson, who aspired to give Labour the same sort of centrist image, met the first requirement of a natural governing leader: he won four out of five general elections in which he led his party, and held the office of prime minister longer than anyone else in peacetime in this century. He was admired by his supporters for his ingenuity and scorned by his enemies as devious. Wilsonian maxims that are best remembered are that a week is a long time in politics, and that he liked to fly by the seat of his pants.[7] This metaphor does not conjure up a picture of the majesty of power; and it was Wilson's misfortune that he was never able to invest his policies with the emotional force and dignity that characterized Hugh Gaitskell, his predecessor as Labour leader.

It was Gaitskell who sought in the most dramatic fashion to induce the party to jettison some of its doctrinal baggage. After Labour had lost its third successive general election in 1959, he wanted to change Clause 4 of the party constitution which refers to "the common ownership of the means of production, distribution and exchange." The association of Labour with a policy of progressive nationalization was one of its principal electoral handicaps, Gaitskell believed; and he was able to point out justifiably that the Labour party really had no intention of actually putting the whole of Britain's industry, trade, and commerce into public ownership. To acknowledge in cold blood such a departure from the socialist faith was more than the party activists would stomach. Gaitskell was rebuffed, though he was to triumph in subsequent intra-party battles. On this, as on other occasions, he imparted the air of a moral crusade to a pragmatic proposal.

What the course of events would have been if Gaitskell had not died suddenly and prematurely at the beginning of 1963 is the great might-have-been of British postwar politics. His death was without doubt one of the most significant events of the entire era.[8] Wilson, in a very different style, and arousing very different emotions, also sought to lead Labour away from the outdated dogma of its past. The policy of public ownership was relegated to a subordinate place, though steel was renationalized under the Wilson government; and there was no attempt to fight the battle of Clause 4 over again. Wilson regarded this fight as an inadvisable wrangle over the symbol rather than the substance of policy: what he termed, disparagingly, the theology of Labour politics. He placed emphasis upon planning the economy as a whole, public and private, upon developing regional policy, and upon a series of government incentives and regulations intended to encourage the efficiency of British industry.

Wilson's program was largely an extension of what had been begun by the Conservative government under Macmillan; but Labour went farther down the road of detailed intervention than the Conservatives would have gone. The party political war continued unabated—perhaps even with additional ferocity because of the personal mistrust that so many Conservatives felt toward Wilson —but the underlying consensus remained. The assumptions on which both sides based their policies were not greatly different. If the consensus remained throughout much of this period, however, it did not yield results that were satisfactory either to the Labour Party or to the country at large. Wilson's premiership (1964–70, 1974–76) was characterized by a sense of economic failure and, in consequence, by the frustration of many other policies.

The first serious attempt to challenge the postwar consensus was made by the Heath government which was swept into office by the Conservative victory in 1970. That administration began with the commitment to renounce a managed incomes policy for the economy as a whole, and instead, for the control of inflation, to rely upon a combination of fiscal and monetary restraint and upon the example to be set by the government in pay negotiations as the employer in the public sector. Inefficient firms in the private sector would not be rescued by an indulgent government's keeping them alive on public money so as to prevent an increase in unemployment. Companies would have to stand on their own feet. And the excessive power of the unions was to be curbed by new legislation on industrial relations.

The Industrial Relations Act was placed on the statute book in 1971—with ultimately disastrous results, as it engendered a new bitterness between government and the unions without actually doing much to limit the power of the unions in practice. Most of the other elements of the rigorous Heath approach were reversed in what became known as the U-turn of 1972. Faced with the alarming phenomenon of rapidly mounting unemployment, the government discarded monetary restraint. Public money was poured out in an attempt to succor flagging companies and industries. In order to prevent this policy from being sharply inflationary, the government then took refuge in a statutory incomes policy

97

for the whole economy. The previous consensus had apparently been established all the more firmly by the dramatic failure to overturn it.

The Heath government fell in February 1974 because it became embroiled in a conflict with the miners over the very statutory incomes policy that it had originally determined to avoid. The miners refused to accept the limitation on pay increases set by that policy, and went on strike, after initially limiting their production. The government put industry on a three-day week in order to conserve coal stocks, but the country was still faced with the danger that energy supplies would run out because workers were picketing electricity power stations in sympathy with the miners. Coal stocks had not run out, but fresh supplies could not be moved into the power stations because of the picketing. In the hope of escaping from this impasse, and of bringing renewed public pressure on the miners to reach a settlement, Heath called a general election—though reluctantly and a little later than some of his closest advisers had proposed. The strategem failed. The election gave no single party an overall majority; but Labour had the most seats, even though the Conservatives won more votes. So Wilson was reinstated in office at the head of a minority government.[9]

Perhaps the strongest feature of Wilson's second period in the premiership was the overt power exercised by the trade unions. Wilson, in his turn, proclaimed before and after taking office in 1974 that there would be no compulsory incomes policy. Instead, there would be a social contract with the trade unions. In return for the government's taking special account of union wishes over a range of policies—not just industrial relations policy, though paying particular attention to that—the unions would keep their wage demands to reasonable limits. The first part of this contract was applied more noticeably than was the second. The Industrial Relations Act, which the unions hated, was repealed and subsequently replaced by legislation even more favorable to the unions than the law had been before 1971. An unusually large increase in retirement pensions was forced on the government by union

98

pressure; and union influence was evident in other fields as well.

There was, nonetheless, a wages explosion, and it led to the most severe bout of inflation that Britain had experienced in modern times. In the summer of 1975 the government—fortified by its election victory in October 1974, which gave it a small overall majority, and by its success in June 1975 in the referendum confirming British membership in the European Economic Community—brought in a new voluntary incomes policy and threatened a statutory measure if the voluntary policy was disregarded. The policy was not disregarded. It had the blessing of the union leaders—indeed, its precise form was largely devised by the most powerful of them, Jack Jones, the general secretary of the Transport and General Workers—and, for the first three annual phases —as they were known—it was observed far more widely than most people had expected. For the first two years the policy had the explicit backing of the union leaders, and the third phase had at least the tacit acquiescence of most of them. The rate of price inflation was brought down to single figures, much to the relief of the government, which had invested much political capital in the claim that it would achieve this goal.

It was the attempted fourth phase that was to prove disastrous for the Labour government, by then under the leadership of James Callaghan who succeeded Wilson as Prime Minister in April 1976. For this phase (1978–79) the government sought to halve to 5 percent the level of annual pay increases permitted under the policy. This was too rigorous for union leaders to accept. Most of them had quietly gone along with the previous round's ceiling of 10 percent, though opinion among their rank-and-file members had made it impossible for them openly to approve it. The proposed reduction in the ceiling provoked a revolt throughout the trade union movement, where there was mounting discontent over the restrictions already in operation. These were believed to be not only holding down the level of pay overall but also to be squeezing the traditional differentials between one group of workers and another.

The government suffered a great deal from the public outrage at the disruption caused by the industrial disputes that followed during the winter of 1978–79. Garbage was left uncollected, dead bodies went unburied, supplies were denied to some hospital patients, food stocks were jeopardized, and so forth. Reports were frequently even more horrifying than was the experience, but the political effect was not weakened by journalistic alarmism. Not only was the government damaged by natural public indignation; but one of its strongest claims to electoral support was gravely undermined—the claim that only Labour knew how to handle the unions.

This factor had much to do with Labour's decisive defeat in the election of May 1979. It might be argued that, even so, the underlying consensus was maintained. The Conservatives, under Margaret Thatcher, who had replaced Edward Heath as leader in 1975, were firmly committed against any formal incomes policy. The Labour government's experience had shown that no government, of whatever party, could hope to implement such a policy, at least for the time being. The Conservatives emphasized firm control of the money supply as the principal instrument of economic management and as the most effective means of curbing inflation. Labour's Chancellor of the Exchequer, Denis Healey, had been pursuing modified monetarist policies. Indeed, in his first speech to the party conference as Prime Minister in 1976, Callaghan had warned that it was an illusion to suppose it possible for the country to spend its way out of unemployment—a sharp reversal of traditional Labour attitudes, and a signal that his government would be middle-of-the-road and undoctrinaire in economics.

Both parties were to some extent reacting in much the same way to the pressure of events, as they have consistently done in the postwar world, allowing for time lags and differences of style. Even the Heath government's controversial Industrial Relations Act— one of the most hated pieces of legislation in modern times—was proceeding along a path that the previous Labour government had sought to travel. Mr. Wilson and his Secretary of State for Employment, Barbara Castle, had wished to legislate along the lines of their 1969 White Paper, *In Place of Strife,* whose proposals did not differ much in substance from the Industrial Relations Act.[10] Mr. Wilson and Mrs. Castle were thwarted by union pressure, which built up such formidable resistance in both the Cabinet and the parliamentary Labour party that it became impossible to go ahead. By 1979, however, both major parties had begun to retreat from the postwar consensus. Indeed, the Conservatives made more than a beginning and fought the 1979 election on a program that broke openly with the consensus. The central fact of British politics in the late 1970s was that the economy sustaining this consensus was no longer delivering the goods. This fact had critical consequences for both main parties.

THE LABOUR PARTY

Britain's Labour party is often regarded by observers in other countries as essentially ideological, as thirsting to create the socialist state. This impression is no doubt derived from a literal reading of the party constitution and from close attention to party rhetoric. The reality is less clear-cut. The party grew out of the Labour Representation Committee, which was formed in 1900 to secure, as its name suggests, representation in Parliament for what was in effect a combination of trade unions and organizations representing various socialist societies up and down the country. This mixed parentage has characterized the party throughout its life. There are the trade unions, eager to defend and to further their sectional interests; there are those who wish to build a new society; and in between are those who have no socialist blueprint in their pockets but seek change in order generally to protect the underdog. The dividing lines are naturally blurred. There are ardent socialists in the trade unions and earthy pragmatists elsewhere in the party. But it is reasonable to look upon the Labour party as an amalgam of

101

those who want it simply to look after the special interests of working people and of those who want it to transform society—with a good many who harbor generalized feelings that Labour needs to be an idealistic party with a sense of purpose.

Throughout the party's life the trade unions have been the dominant influence, largely because they have the money, the organization, and the votes at the annual conference. They are for the most part skeptical, even resentful, of intellectuals with highbrow ideas. This practical bias is reinforced by the average Labour voter, who wants a better deal for workers and their families but is easily frightened off by grandiose projects that seem impracticable. The ideological Labour politicians tend on the whole to be electoral handicaps who, in partisan debate, draw criticism upon the entire Labour party. It is therefore mistaken to think of the Labour party simply as an instrument for putting socialist nostrums into practice. This is what an important section of the party wishes to do, but it is not yet the prevailing ethic—even though the word "socialism" is obligatory for the rhetoric of all sections of the party. Neither is it the whole truth, though, to see Labour as merely a political vehicle for the trade unions. There will be frustration within the party if its members feel that it is not serving some cause; many of these people went into politics to change society, not just to manage it. On the other hand, there will also be dissatisfaction if the party seems to lose its sense of political realism.

These often conflicting ends were largely reconciled in the 1950s by the social democratic revisionist doctrines of Anthony Crosland. We have mentioned how Hugh Gaitskell sought to induce the party to dramatize its awareness of political reality by renouncing the goal of wholesale public ownership. This was more than the party conference was prepared to swallow; but even had Gaitskell been successful, it would by itself have been a negative achievement. Labour would have dropped an outdated doctrine, in which most of its leaders did not themselves really believe and which was antagonizing the electorate; yet it would not have gained the alternative purpose that it needs. This purpose was provided—indeed, had already been provided—by Crosland. In *The Future of Socialism,* published in 1956, Crosland argued that the ownership of industry is under modern conditions no longer the key factor in determining the character of a society.[11] An extension of public ownership might be the right policy in particular instances, but it had to be justified on practical grounds. What mattered above everything else was the pursuit of equality, by which Crosland meant more than equality of opportunity or the wider distribution of income. He wanted both of these, but he was seeking a wider economic and social equality in a broad sense. He had in mind a greater equality in the distribution of property, in the educational system, in class and status in industry and in private life. In order to achieve these aims, he believed there should be a wide range of expensive public programs which would entail the transfer of a proportion of the national income from private to public expenditure. This was to be paid for out of increased growth—a relatively easy assumption in the confident days of the 1950s.

This program was certainly not what the Conservatives were offering; but it was more moderate than conventional socialist doctrine and was well within the terms of the postwar consensus. Crosland put his faith in an activist government, with ambitious programs financed by public money, at a time when the Conservatives were themselves increasing public spending, even if more slowly than Crosland advocated. Moreover, Crosland gave low priority to public ownership, which was no longer to be an article of faith. These revisionist ideas, propounded in his book and developed by Crosland in his subsequent writing, became the doctrine of the dominant right wing of the party. He gave a generation of moderate socialists their philosophy.

It was founded, however, upon a mistaken assumption that there would be sufficient growth to provide for a relatively painless transfer of resources from the private to the public sector in order to pay for his social and industrial programs. This growth was not to be. Crosland himself was later to lament:

Under conditions of slow growth, efforts to achieve these transfers inevitably provoke inflation. For since they cannot come from the fruits of rapid growth, they must come from higher taxation of existing incomes. But higher indirect taxes put up prices; higher direct taxes provoke compensating claims for higher money wages and salaries. In our slow-growth economy the shift of resources away from personal consumption has harshly exacerbated the problem of inflation.[12]

Resistance to high taxation has become even stronger since Crosland wrote these words. By the time Labour went out of office in May 1979, a higher proportion of the working population were paying income tax than ever before. This was partly because of the ever-increasing burden of public expenditure and partly because over a period of years inflation had raised money incomes to the point where ever more poor people were brought within the tax net, even though their incomes were not worth as much in real terms as they would have been when the tax rates were originally set. In 1976 a rebellion was led by two left-wing Labour M.P.'s, Audrey Wise and Jeffrey Rooker; and it forced the Labour Chancellor, Denis Healey, to accept the principle of indexing income tax allowances. Personal taxation had ceased to be the process by which those who were well-off paid for the social wage of those who were not; it was seen increasingly by many solid Labour supporters as a process by which those who worked for their living paid for the benefits of those who did not work. In such an atmosphere Croslandite revisionism could not possibly flourish.

That perception might not have mattered too much if Labour's record in office had been generally considered to be successful, if its had been a story of competent stewardship even without bold reforms. In the fourteen and one-half years following the thirteen of Tory rule in 1964, until Margaret Thatcher entered Downing Street in 1979, Labour was in office for eleven years. Long periods in government frequently drive the ideology out of politicians. So much of their working lives is spent in responding to events, in putting out fires, that it is hard for all except the most zealous conceptualizers to tailor their responses to fit their political philosophy. Such has been the experience not only of Labour politicians. Sir Keith Joseph, for long the chief theoretician of the Conservative right wing, lamented that he did not really act as a Conservative when he was Secretary of State for Social Services throughout the Heath government. After he returned to government, in 1979, as Secretary of State for Industry, he became more pragmatic again.

When Labour lost in 1970 and in 1979, ministers left office uncomfortably aware that they had lost not only the confidence of the electorate but touch with their own supporters—that they had, in other words, failed to meet the requirements either of good government or of the Labour tradition. That charge could be made with more force in 1970: the stamp of failure did, indeed, mark that government. The record of Labour from 1974 to 1979 was more mixed and can be divided into three periods. The first lasted from 1974 until the beginning of the first phase of the incomes policy in the summer of 1975 which followed close upon the referendum confirming British membership in the EEC. This period saw inflation out of control and the government apparently at the mercy of the unions. The second period went on from 1975 until Callaghan's decision in October 1978 not to call an election that autumn as expected. During these three years the government seemed to be managing the country's affairs rather well. Britain's underlying problems were not solved; but inflation was much reduced, the unions were cooperative in moderating their wage claims, and there was an air of competent management. The third and final period—the bitter winter of 1978–79—saw the unions in revolt, wage inflation soaring ahead again, industrial and social disruption, and the crumbling authority of the Prime Minister and his government.

In Britain, as in the United States, it has for long been one of the cherished maxims of political analysis that electoral victory goes to the party that holds the middle ground. Britons, like Americans, prefer their political leaders to be reassuring. This concept does depend for its relevance upon a measure of agreement about where the middle ground lies, about what is moderate and what is extreme. The idea is that the battle is fought along a narrow strip of territory at each end of which one of the major parties has its own relatively secure support.[13] Between these ends are the floating voters—those who change parties and those who may not vote at all but who, when they do vote, always cast a ballot for the same party; and the party that manages to activate and capture most of these voters is the party that wins. Each party must therefore seek to move toward the center, while keeping the allegiance of its traditional supporters and maintaining a sufficient distinction between itself and its opponent. On this analysis, if the more left-wing party moves farther to the left, the right-wing party should also shift to the left in order to capture more of the middle ground —while the gap between it and the opposition remains large enough to persuade its customary supporters to continue voting for it. The converse applies if the right-wing party moves to the right. If neither party moves toward the extreme, then both parties have to indulge in complicated maneuvers over a small patch of ground in the center. This stately dance does not make for ideological politics, but it may not necessarily be bad for the country.

If the 1979 election had been fought for the middle ground represented by the postwar consensus, Labour would in all probability have won. In the course of the Labour campaign, there was little talk of further nationalization. Labour no longer looked so capable of keeping the unions quiet; but party leaders could maintain that if the unions were restive, the Conservatives would be even worse at handling them. Labour was proposing to keep up all the activities that the public now expected of government, while much of its campaign consisted of pointing to the fields from which it was alleged that the Conservatives would withdraw. And in personal terms James Callaghan was far more popular than Margaret Thatcher.

Yet Labour did not win. Of the voters 5.2 percent moved from Labour toward the Conservatives—the highest swing in the postwar years, though they still gave the Tories less than an overall majority in the popular vote. However, according to the formula that converts votes in the constituencies into parliamentary seats, the Conservatives controlled the next House of Commons by a majority of forty-three seats over all other parties combined. This was a margin of safety wide enough to assure Mrs. Thatcher of a full five years without a serious parliamentary challenge to the existence of her government. Even given the strong propensity of by-elections to go against the government, they do not occur with sufficient frequency to disturb a majority of forty-three.[14]

According to the conventional view of elections as battles for the middle ground, the Conservatives did not win the 1979 general election. Labour lost it. It was palpably in the air that the Labour government had become tired; its formula for industrial peace had been tried and tried again and at long last was found wanting.

THE CONSERVATIVE PARTY

Meanwhile, the leadership of the Conservative party displayed little interest in contesting the traditional middle ground. In a speech to the Conservative party conference in 1975, Mrs. Thatcher's close associate on economic matters, Sir Keith Joseph, rejected the concept of the middle ground in favor of what he termed the "common ground."[15] Sir Keith is something of a puzzle to political analysts because, although he has one of the most acute minds in British politics, he sometimes has difficulty in making his meaning clear. So it was on this occasion. The distinction he drew seemed to be meaningless, or at least too subtle to matter in the world of practical politics. But, in fact, he was indicating the lines along which the Conservatives would henceforth seek to operate. He was serving notice that they were abandoning the postwar consensus.

On some matters the Conservatives had innovated without materially disrupting this consensus. The introduction of commercial

107

television by the Conservative government in the mid-1950s was bitterly contested, but it proved so popular that no government would now dare to abolish it. When restrictions on Commonwealth immigration were first imposed in 1962, the principle was vigorously opposed; but no administration would now risk abolishing controls, and the only question is how they should be applied. The sale of council houses to their tenants is still a matter of contention in some quarters, but it is fast on the way to becoming accepted.

The fresh direction in which the Conservatives determined to strike out meant a sharp turn economically to the right and entailed reducing the role that government has played in Britain throughout the postwar period under administrations of both parties. There were to be greater incentives for individuals to work harder and to spend their money as they thought fit, not as the state thought best. To carry out this policy meant cuts in personal taxation and in public expenditure. There were to be new techniques of economic control, with no managed incomes policy and reliance instead upon strict control of the money supply and upon enforcing cash limits for the nationalized industries. These techniques were expected to curb the capacity of employers in both the private and the public sectors to pay inflationary wage increases. If the unions insisted on pay raises for which the money was not available, then these raises could be had only at the cost of increasing unemployment. The size of the public sector was to be reduced, at least marginally for a start. Less would be done for ailing industries in the private sector. There would be changes in industrial relations law, but the new Conservative attitude to the trade unions was modified, and confused, by the differences between Prime Minister Thatcher and her Secretary of State for Employment, James Prior.

Some of these proposals had been heard before when the Heath government took office, but on this occasion the withdrawal from collectivism was preached with more zeal and more ardent conviction, and was a distinct victory for one of the two schools of thought within the modern Conservative party. The pragmatic tradition among Conservatives—the school of trimmers and bal-ancers, who are unideological on principle—has already been men-tioned. They have been in the ascendant for most of the postwar period, indeed for most of this century. Between the wars they were represented most notably by Stanley Baldwin; and in the postwar years, by Harold Macmillan and R. A. Butler. Churchill never showed much interest in Conservative philosophy and was, on the whole, enough of a pragmatist to be put in this school.

There has for years, however, been a contrary tendency within the party—a tendency that owes more to the Gladstonian Liberal tradition of the nineteenth century than to any other.[16] This second school of thought has always argued that more of the national income should be left in the pockets of the people, that there should be less state provision of services, less government intervention in industry, and that as far as possible decisions should be left to the free market.

When, after the First World War, Labour took over from the Liberals as one of the two principal British parties, many erstwhile Liberals joined the Conservatives. In later years many who, in an earlier period, would have joined the old Liberal party have gone into the Conservative party because the British electoral system—first-past-the-post rather than proportional representation—gives little hope of power, or even of large representation, to any party outside the big two. The Conservatives thus expanded beyond the old Tory base into a broad non-socialist party.

In recent years this second tendency was represented most effec-tively by Enoch Powell while he was still a Conservative, and by Margaret Thatcher and Keith Joseph. It has consistently exerted influence on Conservative policies and attitudes, but it was never dominant in the postwar period until Margaret Thatcher was elected leader in February 1975. For a time while he was leader Edward Heath allied himself with this tendency, but he never really adopted it wholeheartedly and has since been considered one of the most conspicuous of the pragmatists. The rise to ascendance of the free marketeers in the Conservative party was partly a coincidence, since Margaret Thatcher did not win the leadership on philosophy alone; it was attributable even more to the failure of the postwar consensus to reverse Britain's progressive decline. When a nation suffers a succession of defeats, it is just as likely as a football team to look favorably upon a possible change of managers. The question presented to Britain by the 1979 election was whether the Conservatives, in breaking away from the old consensus, would be able in time to lay the basis for a new one.

The fact that the Conservatives seemed an exceptionally partisan administration when first elected is beside the point. So, too, seemed the Attlee government when it took office in 1945—and for quite a while after. Like the Attlee government, the Thatcher administration is faced with the problem of establishing lines of policy that, however contentious they are when introduced, can later become so generally accepted that successor governments may modify but not reverse them. The election itself provided only a partial guide to the future. One of the most important reasons for Labour's loss is that its traditionally large lead among the skilled working class was much eroded.[17] There was no longer the old attachment to such policies as redistributive taxation—which nowadays redistributes income away from, not toward skilled workers—or to expansion of the welfare state or government intervention in the economy. Bureaucracy had become still more unpopular. There was even less support for further nationalization. The sale of council houses to their tenants, with the inevitable consequence of a declining municipal housing sector, was much favored. And resentment against the power of the unions had become still stronger, even though most skilled workers belong to one.

This trend of thinking among skilled workers was in step with the general movement of opinion among the population as a whole and encouraged belief in the existence of a basis for a new consensus. Such an assumption needs, however, to be qualified in two respects. The first is that the electorate collectively is often as illogical as most of us are individually: it is one thing to clamor for cuts in taxation; it is another to favor specific reductions in public expenditure to pay for them. This public schizophrenia has been most evident in recent attitudes toward the trade unions. The electorate wants a government that will curb the power of the unions, but not a government that will get into a fight with them. It wants to win a war without waging it. The trend is to favor less government intervention, both in the economy and in the lives of the people generally; but any government that fails to provide prosperity will still be held responsible. In any case, the Conservative victory must be attributed quite considerably to the public's sense of outrage over union behavior the previous winter—for which Labour was held accountable both as the party of the unions and as the government of the day—as well as to these deeper currents of opinion.

The second qualification follows naturally from this last point. British political opinion has become increasingly volatile in recent years—as is evident in the rapid switches of support between the main parties, not only in by-elections and opinion polls between general elections, but also in the general elections themselves. The swing of opinion in the Conservatives' favor in 1979 was greater than at any other general election since 1945. Another sign of volatility, or at any rate of the weakening of traditional allegiances, has been the greater strength of the smaller parties.

These did not do so well in 1979—with 19 percent of the vote —as they had done in the elections of 1974, when they captured 25 percent of the vote. In terms of seats, the Liberals dropped from thirteen in October 1974 to eleven in 1979; the Scottish Nationalists, from eleven to two; and the Welsh Nationalists, from three to two. But in both seats and votes the smaller parties did better in 1979 than in all other postwar general elections but 1974. Elsewhere we have examined the special reasons for the ebb and flow of Scottish and Welsh nationalism and for the breakaway of the Ulster Unionists from the British Conservatives. The extent of any Liberal rise is largely a measure of public dissatisfaction with the two main parties.

POLITICAL VALUES

THE LIBERAL PARTY

There are certainly positive reasons for voting Liberal. The party has had a good record in the postwar years for developing new policies. It was the first to advocate British membership in the EEC. Its influence on the Labour government during the period of the Lib-Lab parliamentary pact from the spring of 1977 to the end of the summer in 1978 was limited but generally healthy.[18] The Liberal party stands today, above all, for breaking down the barriers and the antagonisms between the two sides of industry which have bedeviled the British economy.

Yet, ever since the Liberals ceased to be one of the two major parties, they have been confronted by the fact that a vote for the Liberals is normally a wasted vote. They have had no chance of forming a government and, in most constituencies, little prospect of electing a member of Parliament. Their fortunes could revive only if established voting patterns were broken down. In the early 1960s Jo Grimond, who led the party from 1956 to 1967, sought to create what he termed a realignment of the left in British politics. This realignment could be achieved by the Liberals either replacing Labour as the principal party of the left or merging with Labour's right-wing to form a new party. Nothing came of this strategy then, partly because Labour disappointed its critics by obstinately refusing to split, and partly because most Liberal voters are disenchanted Conservatives who do not want to support any party on the left of British politics. Disgruntled Tories have been prepared to vote Liberal, whereas dissatisfied Labour supporters have tended either to swallow their grievances or to abstain.

Recent evidence does suggest that the solid Labour vote is weakening. The Liberals elected three M.P.'s in 1979 from formerly Labour constituencies—an unusually strong showing. Moreover, nowhere in British politics are allegiances so clearly prescribed by social class as they once were. The geographical division, on the

112

other hand, is becoming sharper, with Labour's strength more than ever concentrated in the industrial areas of the north, and with the Conservatives dominating the expanding conurbations and country towns of the south.[19] The old social stereotypes still apply in broad terms, with middle-class voters voting mostly for Conservatives and working-class voters for Labour candidates; but exceptions are now numerous. The Conservatives have not been a single-class party; in the 1970s sometimes half of their vote came from the working class; and although Labour continues to be more of a class-bound party and to draw most of its support from the working class, its proportion of votes from the middle class was not reduced in 1979.

A NEW CONSENSUS

Restiveness among voters could provide the conditions either for a generation of political oscillation, with no government confident of maintaining its support whenever a cloud passed over the sun, or for the beginning of a new consensus. The latter outcome would have profound importance for the conduct of British affairs. It would not guarantee everlasting Conservative rule any more than the establishment of the Attlee consensus put Labour in office in an earlier decade—when first Churchill, then Eden, and finally Macmillan all won election victories for the Conservatives, and with increasing majorities. Within the Conservative Party, however, a new consensus would presumably confirm the free marketeers in their ascendancy. Such consensus is by no means assured; there remains a powerful group of pragmatists within the Thatcher Cabinet, and their tradition, with its strong roots within the party, can never be discounted.

Within the Labour Party the effects of a new consensus would be more subtle. In opposition Labour is traditionally volatile and

113

strife-ridden. The contemporary struggle for power is between a right wing led by those experienced in managing the government on the basis of the old consensus, but without many fresh ideas, and a left wing offering an alternative strategy outside that consensus. This strategy would consist of increased public ownership and public control, and more public money would be given to private companies for investment in accordance with planning agreements among employers, unions, and government, within a seige economy protected by import controls. So long as there is a prospect of the Labour Party dominated by its right-wing leaders being returned to office simply in order to manage competently where the Conservatives had brought confusion, there is relatively little pressure on Labour's right wing to develop a new philosophy. But they would have to react under two conditions. First, if the Conservatives do succeed in establishing a new consensus, then it would not be enough for any Labour leader simply to offer efficient management along the old lines. The most likely development then would be a new right-wing Labour doctrine—of which there have already been some signs—relying less upon state collectivism and concentrating upon the promotion, within the state, of smaller entities with which individuals can identify more readily.[20]

The second condition favoring the resurgence of a systematic ideology of social democracy is if the left wing of the Labour party were to gain in strength sufficiently to force upon the managerial and pragmatic members of the center and right wing the realization that they can neither win their battle for control of the party, nor compete successfully in a general election, without making common cause with the intellectuals of the Labour right wing. Party membership in the constituency Labour parties has shrunk scandalously at a time when constituency parties—dominated by the left—are seeking to extend their power within the party. In order to win their battle, Labour's center and right must mobilize their supporters within the unions and the constituencies—perhaps an impossible task without a more philosophically grounded ideology than those that the pragmatists who ran the Callaghan government, and who still run the parliamentary Labour party, are accustomed to provide.

What if a new consensus is not established? What if the hostility to Thatcher policies remains too great? Then the old consensus would be renewed—and strengthened because there would apparently be no alternative to seeking accomodations with the dominant forces in British society. The attempt to change the basis of the game would have been proved impossible. Such at least would be the general wisdom. So, one way or the other, the fate of the Thatcher experiment may well be a turning point for Britain.

CHAPTER 5

Parliament and Government:
An Elusive Balance

Almost all problems that a society like Britain faces filter in one way or another through Parliament; but they are defined in and through Parliament by the government. So understanding the relationship between Parliament and government is critical to any assessment of the long-term prospects for the United Kingdom. The essence of the American political system is the separation of powers among the President, the Congress, and the Supreme Court. The essence of the British system is the sovereignty of Parliament. Parliament can enact whatever laws it wishes. These will be approved by the monarch and never challenged by the courts. The proper interpretation of a law may be questioned in the courts, but the will of Parliament may not be.

There is no separation of powers in Britain, and governments operate by exercising the authority of Parliament. But Parliament as an institution does not possess the supremacy in practice that it does in constitutional theory. Parliament is a constitutional giant; but under normal circumstances the government of the day

116

is the brains of Parliament, a small part of the body determining how the limbs of the giant shall be moved.[1]

The anxiety that is frequently expressed by political observers about the United States is that Congress may possess too much power and hence is able to frustrate the purposes of constructive government. A President may propose what he chooses—an energy program or an international treaty—but there can be no guarantee that he will be able to get it approved. Nor can there be any assurance that, in setting its will against his, the Congress will have taken thought to relate one policy to another in order to produce a coherent whole. From a British perspective, the danger in the United States is that the processes of decision making may be negative and fragmented because the practical authority of the executive branch is inadequate. The anxiety about British government is precisely the other way round: that Parliament as an institution plays a less powerful role than is desirable from the standpoint of democratic accountability and even of governmental effectiveness.

A government can remain in office only for as long as it can command the confidence of the House of Commons. Confidence does not mean that the House must approve each of the specific policies that the government puts forward; but certain policies are so central to the operation of government that if ministers cannot get them through, they cannot effectively run the country. The annual Finance Bill is a prime example. It is up to the government itself, however, to determine which policies actually are so critical that if they are denied by the House of Commons, then the government must fall.

Under the normal circumstances of a majority government, this principle puts immense power in the hands not of the House but of the government of the day. When a majority of members of Parliament belong to its own party, leaders of the government know that they can be defeated only if there is a rebellion within their ranks. No M.P. wishes to incur the odium of bringing down

117

his or her own government, quite apart from the reluctance of those with marginal seats to fight any more elections than necessary. These basic facts produce the party discipline for which the British Parliament is so famous.[2]

Indeed, no majority government has fallen on a vote of confidence in this century. James Callaghan was defeated on a motion of censure in March 1979, and Ramsay MacDonald lost in October 1923 when he turned a vote on a minor contentious issue into a matter of confidence. But both in 1923 and in 1979 it was a minority government that was defeated. Each government lost, not because its own members defected, but because the other parties combined to bring it down.[3]

It is therefore most unusual for a British government to be brought down in Parliament, and unknown for a majority government to suffer such a fate this century. Ministers in a majority administration know that if they make an issue a matter of confidence, they are virtually guaranteed to win the vote in the House of Commons. This does not mean that they turn a great many items into formal votes of confidence. They have generally not needed to do so. The possession of this power in reserve strengthens the hands of the Whips in requiring conformity, especially as there has developed the convention that, in order to govern successfully, a British Cabinet has to be able to get just about all its policies through Parliament.

The convention has not always applied in recent years. The Labour government of 1966–70 had to give up its intention to reform the law on industrial relations in accordance with its white paper, *In Place of Strife*—though the government was thwarted then principally by pressure from the unions, so that ultimately a majority of the Cabinet itself was not prepared to push ahead. No bill to implement the white paper was ever presented to Parliament. That government was also unable to enact its bill to reform the composition of the House of Lords. The Heath government of 1970–74 was balked by its backbenchers on a number of occasions, though never on an issue of front-rank importance. It was different for most of the time under the Callaghan government, as will be explained shortly, but Callaghan's was a period of minority rule. Under a majority administration, party discipline has usually been so strong that it has been possible, with only a few exceptions, to enforce the convention that a government is entitled to have its way in Parliament.[4]

Such a convention is congenial to ministers and destructive of the powers and responsibilities of Parliament. It is the task of Parliament not simply to sustain governments in office, to pass the laws, and to vote the money that ministers wish. Parliament is supposed to exercise its judgment in examining the proposals and scrutinizing the activities of government. The failure of Parliament for most of the modern era has lain in its weakness in providing proper checks to the power of successive governments of all parties —a weakness that has been all the more notable because the powers that governments have been exercising are derived from Parliament.

Parliament has, as a general rule, given such automatic approval to ministerial proposals that governments have not been forced to take account of parliamentary opinion to any significant extent. Yet even in this weakened condition, Parliament is not wholly negligible. Parliamentary opinion matters for individual ministers. The minister who is rising, or whose grasp upon the office he holds is insecure, will care a great deal about parliamentary opinion because it can affect his standing in the government. Prime Ministers like to feel that their ministers can create a good impression in the House and command the support of their party. Parliament is also a sounding board for the parties' rival points of view, which are picked up by journalists, broadcasters, and other opinion makers who traffic with friends and sources in Parliament—even if they do not percolate so surely to the wider public as traditionalists believe. Performance in the House of Commons has acquired a new dimension since April 1978, when parts of its proceedings began to be broadcast. These are, however, all subsidiary forms of influence. With the exceptions mentioned, governments have not had

119

to worry much about the opinion of Parliament because its decisions could be taken for granted; and therefore Parliament has not been sufficiently effective either in guiding or in scrutinizing the policies of government.

From the spring of 1976 until the fall of the Labour government three years later, Britain had the relatively unusual experience of a minority administration. Labour also ruled as a minority government between the two general elections of February and October 1974. Before that, one has to go back to 1931 for another example of minority government. The latest spell was notable for the changes in attitudes and customs that accompanied it. Some of these can be attributed directly to the circumstances of the time and could not be expected to last beyond it. The significance of others may well last longer.

From 1975 to 1979 the government was defeated on numerous occasions, sometimes on questions of consequence, without making any of them matters of confidence. Successive finance bills were changed, sometimes to the point of significantly altering the Chancellor's budget strategy. The Aircraft and Shipbuilding Bill, nationalizing these two industries, was mauled when ship repairing was removed from its provisions. The Dock Work Regulation Bill did not get through Parliament at all. One bill on devolution was blocked altogether. Another was amended so crucially as to prevent the scheme from being implemented, and ultimately brought about the government's downfall. And there were many other defeats on matters of lesser importance.

With the election of the Conservatives to office on 3 May 1979, the days of minority rule were brought to an end. So the experience of the previous three years may come to be seen as an unusual interlude. There could be no possibility of a majority government of either party tamely accepting some of the rebuffs that Mr. Callaghan and his colleagues had to endure.

Yet it was only after its position had been gravely undermined by events outside Parliament—the hard winter of 1978–79, the wave of industrial disputes, and the failure of the Scottish devolu-

120

tion referendum to produce a clear result—that the Callaghan government was brought down in the House. One of the lessons of the Callaghan era is that British governments can in fact suffer a good many parliamentary defeats without losing their authority. It would be healthy if recognition of this general proposition were to lead to a change in the conventions, so that governments could accept, without loss of face, some defeats on more than matters of detail. Thus, Parliament would be able to perform its task of checking the executive more effectively without the risk of an interminable succession of swift elections. In fact, the risk is slight if only Parliament would recognize it—for the power of dissolution in the hands of a government is for much of the time an idle threat. No government wants to risk the ignominy of being brought down in the House, and a government will generally not make a matter an issue of confidence unless it is sure it can win. That flexibility was an important legacy of the Callaghan years.

Another lesson of the Callaghan era was the growing assertiveness of the backbencher. One indication of this development was that, while some of the government's defeats occurred simply because the other parties had a majority when they combined against it, a good many other defeats—including some of the most important—would not have taken place without dissent among Labour M.P.'s. Nor were these always the same rebellious few. Another indication was the mounting pressure for stronger select committees. The role of the backbencher and the future of select committees are linked, and both are of critical importance to the effectiveness of the contribution that Parliament can make to coping with the problems that Britain, in company with the rest of the Western world, faces today.[5]

POLITICAL VALUES

BACK-BENCH IMPACT

The greater assertiveness of legislators, especially of younger ones, is a trend that is not confined to Britain. It is possibly even more evident in the United States, but it is such a sharp departure from British parliamentary practice in this century that it is of particular significance for Parliament. The principal reason for its development is that a high proportion of new members have come into Parliament in order to make politics their main career, even though they may have another job outside politics. These career politicians are not content to be lobby fodder to anything like the same extent their predecessors were. They came into politics to exercise influence, and they want to do so on the back benches whether or not they are promoted to the front bench. The new mood of assertiveness is obviously less in evidence with a majority government, but it was significant that, little more than six months after being elected with a large majority, the Thatcher government feared that it would have difficulty in getting the renewal of Rhodesian sanctions approved by the House of Commons in November 1979—a fear that influenced its conduct of the Lancaster House negotiations. In May 1980 the government was forced by protests on the floor of the House to renege on an agreement between all the foreign ministers of the European Community to make trade sanctions against Iran retroactive to November 1979.

There are only a few methods by which backbenchers*—even those of the governing party—can have some impact on government policy. There are party committees covering the whole range of government responsibilities, so that most ministers meet fairly frequently with backbenchers of their own party who are interested in their subject matter. The extent of these contacts and of the influence exerted varies a good deal according to the personalities

---

*Members of Parliament who do not belong to the government or to the leadership of the opposition.

of the minister and the committee chairman. It is customary for a minister to sound out his party committee in broad terms before bringing forward significant departures in policy. These committees are therefore a useful means of consultation. An able and ambitious chairman can use his position as a helpful launching pad for the projection of his views—and indeed of himself. The Labour party's right-wing Manifesto Group and left-wing Tribune Group have both considered it worth their while to organize active campaigns for the chairmanship of these committees. Nonetheless, they are advisory bodies at best, so it would be an exaggeration to claim that they are sources of consistent power and influence.

Then there is the regular weekly meeting of the full parliamentary party, whether Labour or Conservative. There is a slight party difference between the parties here. Ministers are members of the Parliamentary Labour party and can attend all meetings. The Conservative 1922 Committee is a committee of the whole party when in opposition; but when the party is in government, it is a committee of backbenchers only. Ministers then attend by invitation. But both these groups can be regarded as essentially meetings of the backbenchers of the respective parties.

Clearly, in a gathering of this sort, it is not possible to discuss every item of policy on the current agenda. There are the constraints of time; and a meeting of more than two hundred, sometimes more than three hundred, people cannot be expected to have the sustained interest to examine every detail of legislation and executive action. If, however, there is any particular question on which a large section of the party feels strongly, a grievance can be aired at these meetings. The other way in which pressure can be brought to bear is difficult for anyone to appreciate who has not closely watched Parliament in operation for any length of time. Within the palace at Westminster—where the Houses of Parliament meet—a limited number of people congregate day after day, speaking, working, voting together in the lobbies, eating in the dining rooms, drinking in the bars, keeping unsocial hours, waiting there, often late at night, to vote on some critical matter. A club atmosphere, a certain camaraderie, develops; and in this atmosphere ministers can be influenced by what they feel is the general mood of the party. Individual backbenchers can have words with senior ministers in the corridors or the smoking room, without an appointment or any other kind of formality; and it can be valuable to say to such a minister: "I don't like your policy on housing at all, and it's not popular in my constituency. A number of my colleagues here don't like it either." This kind of direct personal influence can be quite effective.

These contacts are, however, by their nature haphazard; and the more structured meetings, whether of committees or of the full parliamentary party, are generally used by ministers as opportunities to take the temperature of the water. The task of scrutinizing the operations of government ought, however, to amount to more than being favorably placed for casual conversation, even with the most eminent minister, or than forming part of a politically sensitized pool of water. It ought to mean monitoring the performance of ministers and the conduct of their departments day by day and week by week. How well equipped are backbenchers to do this?

Roy Mason, who was Secretary of State for Northern Ireland in the last Labour government, tells the story of how when he first entered the House of Commons, the leader of his party, Clement Attlee, gave him two pieces of advice: specialize and stay out of the bars. Most M.P.'s today follow at least the first part of this exhortation. They know that they must concentrate their efforts if they are to speak with passable authority on any subject. It is not easy, though, for a backbencher to acquire the knowledge needed to challenge a minister supported by all the resources of his department. There are other calls upon his time. British M.P.'s are poorly paid compared with the legislators of other countries, and most of those who are not themselves in office have other jobs outside the House of Commons which they combine with their political responsibilities.[6] The demands of their constituencies are increasing as well.

124

Parliament and Government: An Elusive Balance

Most constituency associations or parties require more frequent attendance from a member than in the past—at social functions and political discussions. There has also been an enormous rise in recent years in the number of individual constituents who bring grievances or problems to their M.P. In response to this demand for what is in effect social welfare case work, most M.P.'s hold in their constituencies what they call surgeries—regular office hours for consultation with individuals and groups. This trend for ever more people to bring their difficulties to their elected political representative is apparent in a number of countries in the Western world these days—an indication of the extent to which the activities of government impinge on the lives of individuals, who therefore turn to some political champion for redress of their grievances.[7]

While this may be a significant trend, it does not help M.P.'s to keep an eye on the broader activities of government. They also find it difficult to get sufficient information—not just stray facts but knowledge of the range of considerations that have led the government to adopt a particular policy—to know what alternative policies were examined and what the choices may be for the future. Even if one has all the information one needs, it is a rare backbencher who is well equipped to understand and analyze it in sufficient depth. Since public money provides the backbencher with no more than one secretary, he or she generally lacks specialist advice. Even if one were able to overcome all these obstacles, one would find, unless the new system of select committees becomes influential enough to fill this gap, that there is no appropriate forum where one's judgment and criticism can be expressed so regularly as to bear down upon the government and be considered seriously. Unless one is a privy councillor, which one will not be unless one has served on the front bench or has been the leader of the Liberal party, one's opportunities to speak on the floor of the House are severely limited.

So in practice a member of Parliament specializes not to exercise influence as a good backbencher, but to prepare for the front bench. The young ambitious politician will specialize in order to attract attention and so get a foot on the ministerial ladder.

PARLIAMENTARY QUESTIONS

Of all the instruments for getting information from the government, perhaps the most famous is the parliamentary question. Indeed, among the few things that most foreigners know about the parliamentary system is that there is a question hour. This custom is honored most by those who know it only by repute. In practice it serves two functions. It is the modern political equivalent of the medieval tournament, in the sense that it is an occasion not for the serious examination of issues or for eliciting information in any depth from ministers, but for displaying one's opponents to the greatest possible disadvantage. For this purpose a flash of wit is worth an hour of administrative wisdom. Question time is therefore an opportunity for a fair amount of political knockabout humor and entertainment.

The second function of question time is to enable ministers to produce material that they believe to be generally favorable to the government. Friendly backbenchers are deputed to feed appropriate questions to hungry ministers. In doing so, they both help the government to secure a little useful publicity and reduce the time available for critical examination. What really stifles searching scrutiny, however, is the nature of the occasion. It is possible to hold a minister to account for his conduct of complex policies only by a process of sustained consecutive questioning. Such questioning is impossible across the floor of the chamber in a House of 635 members, when only members of the opposition front bench are allowed more than a single supplementary question, and when it is the custom for the

Speaker to alternate the questioning between government and opposition sides of the chamber.

There are both questions that are put down for oral answers as well as those that obtain a written answer. Written answers enable an M.P. who asks the right questions to elicit a fair amount of factual information from government departments. These answers can be useful as research material, though the extent to which they are informative is at the discretion of the relevant department. An M.P. will not, however, be able to learn the considerations that led the government to pursue a particular line of action. He will not be able to find out what other policies were considered or why they were rejected. So it is virtually impossible by means of questions on the floor of Parliament for a backbencher to engage an unwilling minister in any serious colloquy. The parliamentary question is simply not an effective method of monitoring the activities of government.

COMMITTEES

Because question time and the proceedings on the floor of the House are not adequate as a means of calling the government to account and influencing its policies, there have been attempts in response to back-bench pressure from all parties to develop the parliamentary committee system. For British political observers looking across the Atlantic, there are two features of the American system that are striking.[8] One, of course, is the separation of powers between the executive and the legislature—a feature that, without a total constitutional upheaval, Britain cannot emulate. The other is the extent to which both houses of Congress operate through committees. It would not be realistic to think simply of copying the American committee system insofar as this reflects the elaboration of a constitutional separation of powers. A hybrid is possible, however, as in Germany. Even by the standards of Parliamentary systems in advanced democracies, the committee system at Westminster is underdeveloped; and there is growing interest in developing it, not to subvert the workings of Parliament, but to strengthen them.[9]

To a student of the U.S. Congress, perhaps the fundamental fact about Parliament is its substantive incompetence. The institutionalized capacity for Parliament to chart its own ends, to develop a rounded sense of any policy whatever, is virtually nil. Thus, Parliament contributes little to the substantive education of ministers. The question is what sort and what variety of information is available to ministers when the time comes for them to make the hard decisions they must make in steering the nation. The government normally treats Parliament as an adversary rather than as a potential source of assistance. It is not necessarily wholly disadvantageous, however, even from a minister's perspective, for a parliamentary committee to ride around on his back—taking and developing information on its own, raising questions and issues on its own responsibility.

It is quite conceivable that an able minister could use such a committee as a major means of testing the quality of information and recommendations that come up through the Civil Service hierarchies and get placed in his dispatch box every night. The problem is that the contents of those papers are frequently beyond the capacity of a minister to test or to question in any serious way. He has to take an enormous amount at face value from the Civil Service. It would be much healthier for ministers if they had an opportunity to inquire into some of the premises on which the recommendations that are made by the Civil Service are based. For that purpose the findings and the explorations of parliamentary committees ought to be extremely useful.

Another consideration in the development of committees raises questions about the way in which Parliament presently operates: that is, there is too much blindly adversary activity, too much of the cat-and-dog fight across the dispatch box in the House of

Commons. As a rule, debate is regarded as an occasion to try to embarrass the other side, rather than as an opportunity for Parliament collectively to try to develop policies that address the substance of national problems. Without taking the bite out of the political process, it is worth considering whether the way in which Parliament operates is intellectually restrictive. One of the advantages of developing a committee system is that when M.P.'s of different parties are seated together on a committee, they often, in pursuit of substance, come to attach less importance to their party affiliations than they do on the floor of the House. A certain collective committee knowledge, understanding, and—indeed—spirit develops, as is true even on the weak select committees that existed before the reforms of 1979. This is one of the reasons that some members of parliament fear the development of committees: they wish to maintain a sharply partisan style.[10] It is possible to overindulge this wish.

Strong select committees would inevitably lead to some weakening of party discipline in the House of Commons. The specter of the alleged weaknesses of American congressional parties is commonly invoked by opponents of stronger parliamentary committees. The fact is, however, that in the United Kingdom it would be to the positive advantage of Parliament if party discipline were to be somewhat weakened.

In the course of the last Parliament the increasing assertiveness of backbenchers had one lasting consequence: the establishment of a special Select Committee on Procedure to examine the working arrangements of the House of Commons. This committee published a report in August 1978, recommending the creation of a new structure of committees,[11] so that each government department would be covered by a select committee—with some select committees covering more than one department. The general idea, though, was captured by the term "departmental select committees."[12]

This was not a particularly far-reaching proposal. Although the House of Commons has never operated through committees on the

American scale, it has for years had committees to serve a number of different purposes. First of all, there are standing committees that deal with legislation. Each bill, after it has been approved in principle by the House of Commons and given its second reading —the first reading being a purely formal procedure when the bill is initially presented to the House—is then sent to a standing committee to be debated clause by clause. The standing committee (continuing the symmetrical reversal of congressional terminology) will have been appointed specifically to deal with that bill. It may amend, delete, or add extra clauses so long as it does not change the basic purpose and structure of the bill. When it has completed this task, the committee will send the amended bill back to the full House for the report stage, when such changes as the committee may have made will be considered; and the committee will then be disbanded. All committees reflect the balance of parties in the whole House, so governments customarily have a majority of their own members on committees and for the most part do not suffer from many embarrassing amendments of their legislation. Governments are, however, generally reluctant to reverse at report stage the changes made in committee because of the time this process would consume. So most committee amendments are left unchanged; many, indeed, are proposed by ministers themselves after further reflection on a bill that they may have presented in something of a rush. Thus, standing committees have a limited degree of power, but no enduring existence; and of course they have no specialized staff.

There have also been for many years select committees of various kinds. Some are essentially organizational, such as the Select Committee on Procedure and the Select Committee on Privilege, which looks into any alleged infringement of the rights of the House or of any of its members. Other select committees are designed to enable Parliament to monitor the operations of government. The Public Accounts Committee (PAC) has essentially an auditing function. Its principal task is to ensure that public money is spent honestly, sensibly, and without waste; for the most part it is not concerned with policy. Before the 1979 reforms policy could be examined by the Expenditure Committee, which operated through six subcommittees and concerned itself with the purposes for which money was to be spent.[13] In practice, it could look at just about any aspect of government policy; and an individual subcommittee often chose to study some particular problem or question that attracted its interest. Other select committees were set up at the discretion of the House of Commons from one parliamentary session to the next. At the end of the last Parliament there were four of these: the Nationalized Industries Committee, the Science and Technology Committee, the Overseas Development Committee, and the Race Relations and Immigration Committee. The committee system as a whole was a largely ineffective muddle: some committees or subcommittees covered the work of a particular department; others dealt with subjects that involved a number of departments; and only the PAC and the general subcommittee of the Expenditure Committee carried much weight.

The Select Committee on Procedure's proposals provided for tidying this jumble into a coherent pattern. All government departments were to be covered by a committee—as agriculture, for example, had not been—so that there would be no more overlapping investigations. If the report were to be implemented in full, there would be a number of other improvements. Select committees have traditionally been meagerly staffed: apart from a little secretarial help, most of them have had only one clerk—a civil servant who works for the clerk of the House under the Speaker—and one or two part-time advisers. Only the Public Accounts Committee, which is served by the Comptroller and Auditor General and his Exchequer and Audit Department, has had significantly more staff. The report suggested some strengthening of committee staff, though to nothing like the level of U.S. congressional committees, which not uncommonly have over fifty professional staff workers. Select committees of the House of Commons take oral and written evidence, but they cannot compel a minister to appear before them. Nor can they demand as a right the production of official papers from departments that are headed by a secretary of state, as nearly all the major ones are. The report suggested that select committees should have effective powers to send for people and papers. It is customary for select committees to produce reports, which may from time to time cause a political stir, though the government is not forced to act upon them. Parliament is not even required to debate them, and a good many reports remain undebated and unnoticed. The Select Committee on Procedure proposed that eight days should be set aside in each session for debating these reports.

So the report set out a plan for a new structure of select committees that was designed according to a logical principle and had enhanced powers to collect information and a better chance of bringing their conclusions to the attention of the whole House. The permanent committees would, if they were to be at all successful, build up a shared knowledge of a subject and a collective determination to exercise some influence on the conduct of policy. When the report came out, the Conservatives, who were then still in opposition, accepted its broad principles. Once in office, they implemented the proposals—in part. A new structure of select committees was established; but they were not authorized to compel ministers to give evidence, and no time was set aside for the full House to debate their reports. The new committees have no greater power of decision than had the old ones. They do not even have the limited power over legislation possessed by the ad hoc standing committees. They have none of the control over legislation and public expenditure that enables congressional committees to command the respect and the attention of the executive branch.

This is a point of substance: if parliamentary reform in Britain is to be of consequence, it must be more than a technical adjustment designed to make the wheels of the legislature turn more smoothly, and more than merely a means of giving added scope to frustrated legislators. It ought to be a method of opening up the process of decision making with two objectives in mind. One is to enable more people with a wider range of experience to contribute

132

to the legislative process before a final decision is made. The other objective is to make the process of agreement less automatic and more dependent upon acquaintance with substantive issues. The purpose of a legislature is not simply to pass laws. It is also to contribute a measure of popular consent for those laws that are passed. If a government's proposals have to undergo real evaluation before they are enacted, there is a better chance that impracticalities and unforeseen consequences will be exposed; otherwise, legislation risks being enforced by confused courts on a resentful public. If bills are seen by the public to undergo such a test, there is a better chance that they will command public respect when enacted. It will be obvious that they are more than the product of discussions between ministers and their civil servants. Objections will have been argued out and deliberated upon—not merely hurled across the floor of the chamber in the empty charade of rhetorical debate.

For this purpose to be served, the new select committees would need to be given the powers over legislation now possessed by the present standing committees. The difference would be that these powers would be exercised by committees that were permanently established and could therefore be expected to have a greater knowledge of the subject and a determination to make their judgments on the merits of the issue—not simply according to party convenience. It would also be desirable for select committees to have some powers over public expenditure. They could examine consolidated fund bills, authorizing public expenditure, on exactly the same basis as other legislation.[14] These powers would still leave select committees with much less authority than that possessed by congressional committees. But it is not necessary to emulate American practice in order to give British select committees sufficient political muscle to draw ministers and civil servants into serious dialogue with them.

If this course were taken, it might have another unexpected and desirable effect. In any group of people the person who specializes in the problem that is easily solved has relatively less strength over the long run. It is the person who specializes in solving the most awkward difficulty facing that group who is likely to carry the greater weight in discussion. In a government department at the moment, civil servants have expertise in dealing with its particular subject matter, and they have built up over a period of time a knowledge of the interest groups concerned. The strength of the politicians in the department, the ministers, lies in what is supposed to be their superior judgment in assessing public opinion at large and their greater expertise in dealing with Parliament. If the approval of Parliament can be taken for granted, but the interest groups are potentially awkward, and the technical problems presented are extremely complex, then the relative psychological balance between ministers and civil servants is likely to devolve to the side of the civil servants—not because they are a power-grabbing élite, but because they are dealing with the more difficult parts of the overall problem faced by the department. That advantage is why ministers often hesitate to overrule them. In the longer term, the more awkward Parliament is, the greater the strength that ministers are likely to exercise within their departments. This shift in the balance of advantage would provide a greater sense of democratic accountability.

WHIPS AND BACKBENCHERS

One of the ways in which the government, of whatever party, has interacted with select committees is startling to a transatlantic observer: party managers have in the past been able to change the composition of committees virtually at will, unless individual M.P.'s resisted strongly, which they rarely did. Early in 1978 the Select Committee on Nationalised Industries compelled the British Steel Corporation to disclose its internal financial forecasts for the previous two years, which the corporation had been unwilling to reveal to them. At the time this appeared to be a notable victory for the committee and for the oversight powers of Parliament generally. But when the committee's report—a rather critical one —was subsequently debated in the House, the Labour members of the committee voted with their party colleagues, not with their fellow members of the committee. Moreover, party managers—or whips, as they are known—retaliated by quietly removing from the committee two of the offending Labour members who had dared to embarrass the corporation and the government.[15]

Britons are accustomed, as they look at the operation of their parliamentary system, to see the whips as the dominant force. An individual M.P. has two kinds of pressure upon him. He has pressure from his own constituency party, back home, whose support is of critical importance if he is going to be renominated and re-elected to Parliament. But most M.P.'s go into the House of Commons these days in order to gain office in the government, not simply with the idea of having a useful—or a somnolent—career on the back benches. A good many of them used to be satisfied with such a career in the past. But the once natural back benchers— Tory knights of the shires, men of substance from pleasant rural constituencies who were content just to be in Parliament, and their socialist counterparts, the elderly Labour trade union M.P.'s, who enjoyed being merely spear carriers in the Parliamentary pageant —are declining in number in Parliament. The typical M.P. these days is a career politician looking for promotion to the front bench. If he is to get advancement, he needs the approval of the whips because, certainly at the beginning of his career, their recommendation is likely to be decisive. This is one of the principal reasons for the whips' enormous power, although, as we have mentioned, career M.P.'s on the back benches are much more likely to flex their political muscles than were the passive members of the past.

There are fifteen whips on the government side; formally they are attached to the Treasury. Their principal work is not merely sending out the famous calendar notices with the one, two, or three underlinings, which request, require, or demand, respectively, attendance at votes. Rather, they monitor all the activities of the parliamentary party. Their representatives go to most committee meetings. One of their principal tasks is to make a market in the reputations of their own back benchers. They are continuously monitoring the performance of their party members, not merely in order to keep track of the chances of the next bill's passing, but also, over the longer term, to assess the probabilities of each member's having a career in the future as a minister.

They are the main links between the party leadership and the backbenchers. They transmit the wishes and intentions of the front bench to the backbenchers and, as it were, keep the party in line. They also keep the party leadership informed of opinion as it develops on the back benches—any sense of grievance, any particular ideas, any significant change of attitude. And, third, as we have said, they are talent spotters on behalf of the party leadership. This activity is particularly important for all the young politicians who think that it is of great consequence that their talent be spotted.

The power of the whips alone to control the advancement of members, it can be argued, is a sufficient brake on the prospects of committees to fulfill their potential to be inconvenient to the government. Membership on select committees is now determined not by the Whips, as in the past, but by the Committee of Selection, which had previously been responsible for deciding the composition of standing committees only. The Committee of Selection is nominally elected by the whole House; but, since its members are in practice nominated by the whips, there is dispute over how far this change has really removed the power of the whips over select committees. There is always the danger that the whips will wish to keep off a committee people known to have special knowledge or independent views on a particular subject. If a backbencher is known to be very independent, his knowledge of the subject matter may in fact be a disadvantage so far as his chances of getting on a particular committee are concerned. At least the new arrange-

ment offers some safeguard against the flagrant exercise of this option.

The Committee of Selection is a little sensitive about appearing to be an instrument of the whips. It might well be influenced by the whips in making its original choices, but it would demonstrate to the whole House its lack of independence if it were to remove a member from a select committee against his wishes because he had fallen foul of the whips.

BILL OF RIGHTS

One of the most eloquent criticisms in recent years of the way in which Parliament works has come from Lord Hailsham, who complains that Britain is ruled by what he terms an "elective dictatorship."[16] He believes that all constitutional authority is now in effect vested in the House of Commons, unchecked by the judiciary—which cannot challenge the sovereignty of Parliament—or by the House of Lords, which is too weak nowadays to apply any serious check to the Commons. Within the Commons, virtually total power has passed to the government of the day, which can be elected to office without necessarily having the support of a majority of voters in the country. The Labour government that took office in October 1974 had won the votes of less than 30 percent of the total electorate, but those votes were enough to install it initially as a majority administration.

It was therefore in strict terms an unrepresentative government. Yet even such a government was able to push most of its policies through Parliament, so long as it retained its majority in the House of Commons. According to this analysis, whenever a government is installed in office, it finds virtually no constitutional limit to what it is able to do. Parliament is sovereign; and government, within

Parliament, is able to get its wishes put into effect. Lord Hailsham's analysis does not pay much regard to the greater restiveness of M.P.'s, but it contains a substantial measure of truth, even allowing for his politician's gift for exaggeration.

The problem of an unrepresentative government's being able to push its policies through without serious checks can be met in one of three ways. One is to make sure that no government can easily get its policies through Parliament. Another possible remedy is to make sure that governments cannot take office with a majority of seats in the House of Commons without a majority of votes in the country. This remedy would require reform of the electoral system so as to introduce proportional representation: to ensure that the number of seats held by each party in the House of Commons reflected the number of votes each party won in the election. The third possible remedy is to have greater constitutional checks outside Parliament upon decisions made within Parliament. This would be the purpose of a bill of rights.

The question that must be asked in this connection is, What rights are presently trodden upon by government that would be safeguarded by a codified constitutional bill of rights? The notion of a codified bill of rights in the context of a totally uncodified constitution—as Britain's is—implies that some important rights have been transgressed. This is certainly not obviously the case. Moreover, if it is not the case, one has to think carefully whether codified rights are more capacious—that is, whether they guarantee more rights, more securely—than the custom of maintaining rights without codification.

One of the objections to the current situation is that the various safeguards that exist are spelled out only in a rather haphazard fashion. Either there is protection under the common law, or there is protection in particular statutes that forbid certain conduct. The argument is that a bill of rights would put all this in a coherent and positive form. Rights would be established, rather than the present practice of having prohibitions against conduct likely to infringe on assumed rights.

One school of thought claims that to enumerate rights is to safeguard them; another claims that to enumerate rights is to limit them. The issue can be settled only by reference not to the piece of paper on which the rights are inscribed, but rather to the political climate in which rights are asserted and enforced.

A contemporary proposal under careful discussion in Britain is for the European Convention on Human Rights to be incorporated into British law. As Britain is already a signatory to the Convention, such incorporation would mean transferring a set of moral obligations into legal ones. The judgments of the European Court in respect to the Convention would likewise be given legal authority. Thus, British law would take a further step in the gradual process by which it is becoming Europeanized; also, safeguards that are so far implicit would be codified. Whether civil liberties would be more securely guaranteed is doubtful.

SELECTION OF CANDIDATES

The principal safeguards to political liberties and rights must be sought within the political process itself. We have suggested that a major contribution could be made by continuing the process of parliamentary reform, so that Parliament could in reality provide the check upon the executive that it is supposed to do in constitutional theory. But if that solution is to work, M.P.'s will need to be more independent in spirit than they have customarily been in the past. There are signs, as we have said, that they may be changing in this direction; and it would significantly reduce the power of the whips if M.P.'s could find satisfaction in a parliamentary career without attaining executive office—for example, in the chairmanship of select committees with enhanced influence and prestige.

There would still remain the pressure that could be exerted by the constituency associations. One reason for the much greater sense of independence among senators and congressmen in the United States is that they know that their chances of re-election will depend substantially upon their personal standing with the electorate. The situation is quite different in Britain. Probably something like between 400 and 500 of the 635 seats in the House of Commons can be regarded as safe for one or other major party. In these constituencies, it is often said, a dog with the right label could get elected, even though the appeal of the individual candidate matters more than it once did. An M.P.'s chances of being re-elected will depend upon his being renominated as candidate by the local party; and renomination depends in turn upon how he stands in the eyes of a party caucus often run by a small clique. So M.P.'s may find themselves subject to a disproportionate degree of pressure from a small group of local constituency officers.

To an American, the natural solution to the problem of small cliques dominating the nomination process would be to hold primary elections to determine whom the parties would nominate in each parliamentary constituency. An M.P. would know that he could afford to disregard the views of a few powerful figures in the local party, provided that he stood well in the eyes of the voters; and his public reputation could sometimes be enhanced by taking a bold and independent line in Parliament. Once this new electoral relationship was established between M.P.'s and their constituents, members would be all the more eager to develop their own parliamentary institutions as a means of keeping an eye on, and even influencing the policies of, the government of the day. At the same time, in the British context—where the House of Commons would need to sustain some government for a period of time if there were not to be perpetual elections—it would not change the relationship between Parliament and government to the extent that members would be disinclined to go along with the government on the vast majority of things its ministers wished to do. Primary elections for parliamentary nominations would therefore tend to make Parliament a more independently influential institution without inaugu-

rating a system of checks and balances on the American model.
Under British conditions, however, practical difficulties would
arise. The first difficulty is timing in a country without fixed elections. It is unusual for a Parliament to run its full legally permissi-
ble length of five years in Britain; and an election may be called at
any time with little more than three weeks' notice. It would be
difficult to fit proper primaries within that period of time. This
inconvenience could be avoided by holding primaries for the next
election within a few months of the previous one; but there would
be substantive objections to requiring the parties to choose all their
prospective parliamentary candidates possibly years before the
general election in which they were to stand for office.

There is another, more fundamental, difficulty in the way of
primary elections in Britain. In the United States certain geographical qualifications have to be fulfilled before a candidate can stand
for office. A person wanting to run for the Senate cannot as a
practical matter run in a California primary and then, having failed
to win in it, go off and run in a primary in New York—or perhaps
decide that his chances would be better in Georgia.

These geographical constraints are now constitutionally very
weak. The only requirement is that a member of Congress be a
resident of the state containing the constituency for which he sits.[17]
The requirements for establishing residency used to be stringent,
but today they can be quickly and easily met. There is however, a
political bar: on the whole, citizens of a given state do not like to
elect someone from out of state to be their representative.

In the British system, the representation that matters principally
is not geographical, except for the outlying reaches of Scotland,
Wales, and Northern Ireland. In England somebody who is seeking
a seat in Parliament may try to be nominated for a constituency
in almost any part of the country: one week he will try in the
London area; if he fails there, he may hope to be chosen in Yorkshire; or another seat may come up in the West Country.

It would thus be impossible to have primaries in constituencies
up and down the country with as many as one hundred applicants

for a particular constituency, and with overlapping primary campaigns. The only practical arrangement would be a form of modified primary, with the local constituency election committee choosing a short list for the primary election itself.

Here one encounters another critical distinction between the electoral practices of the United States and Britain. In the United States, to be eligible to vote in the election itself, everyone has to make the deliberate act of registering some time before the election. One can register for a particular party or as an independent; and except in those states where any registered voter can vote in any party's primary, it is those voters who register for a party who can take part in its primaries. The American primary system therefore depends upon the system that has evolved for the registration of voters.

In Britain there is a much simpler procedure for appearing on the electoral roll. It is the legal responsibility of every head of household to fill in a form, which is sent round periodically, and which asks for a list of the names of all those living there who are eligible to vote. The case for this system is that it encourages a higher turnout in elections; whereas in the United States one cannot vote—no matter how interested one may become late in the campaign—unless one has sometime previously made the effort to register. As the British system does not require the individual to register in order to vote, there is no opportunity to compile an official register of supporters of a particular party. It would always be possible to have such a register simply as a qualification for voting in a primary. There is a case for this arrangement in light of the declining memberships of British political parties, particularly the Labour party. As the membership subscription for all British parties is very low, however, it is doubtful that many more people would take the trouble to register for this limited purpose. Much the same result as primary elections might well be obtained by giving the choice of candidate to all paid-up members of a party —not merely in the management committee of the constituency.

142

This is true because party membership dues are low and easily managed by anyone with any political interest.

In the Labour party the normal method of selecting a candidate is through the general management committee, whose size will vary a good deal from one constituency to another. The Conservatives frequently attempt to involve as many people as possible. The initial choice of a short list from names sent on from the Conservative Central Office in London is made by the committee of the association, and then all the people on that short list often appear at a meeting of all paid-up members of the association. The most practical way to democratize the nominating process in Britain would be to make this the standard procedure for both parties, even though it would require a change in Labour party rules.

If all reforms suggested in this chapter were carried out, there would then be the prospect of a new balance between Parliament and the government that would do much to strengthen the political system of the United Kingdom. Parliament would be not simply a constitutional arena where the government works its will but an institution having vitality in its own right.[18] It would be harder for any government to get decisions approved by Parliament; but once that approval was given, decisions would be more than the product of secretive discussions among ministers, civil servants, and special interest groups. And this, we believe, would strengthen both accountability and the popular consent on which democratic government rests.

CHAPTER 6

Public Administration

The nature of British public administration is determined by two factors. Unlike the United States, there is no separation of powers; consequently cabinet ministers simultaneously serve in both the legislative and the executive branches of government. Again unlike the United States, all the top administrative posts throughout the government are customarily filled by members of the established Civil Service.[1]

Because there is a separation of powers in the United States, it is not necessary for members of a President's cabinet ever to have served in Congress. Often they come from other walks of life, have experience in running large organizations, and expect to remain in government for a limited time only. In Britain, on the other hand, cabinet ministers are almost invariably members of either the House of Commons or the House of Lords. They are generally much more experienced politicians than their American counterparts, but have little experience in large-scale administration. In most instances they are content to leave the running of their departments to civil servants.

This difference alone would make the distinction between politicians and administrators in government much sharper in Britain than it is in the United States. A still more important difference is that the leading administrative posts do not change hands when the government passes from one party to another, as is the custom in the United States. The in-and-outer, who moves to and fro between an influential post in government and a law firm or academic life, is a familiar breed in Washington—even if he represents a smaller proportion of the total than mythology suggests. But he is a rare animal in London.

Every time a new government takes over in the United States, a new team has to be put together to run each executive department and agency. Not so in Britain. When the Conservatives won the 1979 election, Sir John Hunt stayed on as Secretary of the Cabinet, probably the most powerful Civil Service post in Britain, just as he had served under the preceding Labour government. He left some months later only because he had reached a fixed retirement age. Each department under the Tories was as a matter of course still run by the officials who had been advising Labour ministers only weeks beforehand.

In the British system—as is true in most parliamentary countries—changing ministers are advised by a continuing bureaucracy, which is responsible for running the administration under only the broadest political supervision. The ministers tend to concentrate on the more important policy questions and on matters that are particularly sensitive politically rather than having to devote time and effort to establishing relationships and effective working patterns. The bureaucracy consists of a professional cadre of highly trained men and women, nearly all of whom spend the whole of their working lives in its service. The Northcote-Trevelyan reforms of 1855 established the principle, which has been observed ever since with few exceptions, of entry on the basis of merit by competitive examination, not by political favor.

Because the most senior administrative posts are customarily filled by the established Civil Service, offering the rewards of tenure and power, it attracts recruits of ambition and ability. The status of the civil servant is consequently far higher in Britain than in the United States. Because it is largely a closed service, it has developed its own subculture, with its own complex and subtle forms of conduct, its own standards of behavior, its own loyalties. Because the bureaucracy continues while governments come and go, each department tends to develop its own line of policy, which will usually be maintained with adjustments from one administration to the next. Because a department is relatively small, it is able to operate on a basis of personal trust, in what by comparison with Washington is a somewhat cozy atmosphere where a person's capacity to inspire confidence among colleagues is one of his or her principal professional assets.

The British Civil Service—recruited by merit examination—is of high intellectual caliber, provides administrative continuity, and, owing to the way its internal standards have developed, offers an assurance of integrity in public life. These are not small virtues. If there were ever a "Watergate" in Britain, the restrictive laws governing the press—both of libel and of contempt of court—make it much less likely that British newspapers would be able to disclose the scandal as effectively as American newspapers did. But the standards of a powerful Civil Service make it much less likely that illegal abuses of executive power like Watergate would ever occur in Britain. Erring ministers would be told by their permanent secretaries that malpractices could not be countenanced: in a society where spirit and custom are still of enormous importance, such abuses would be contrary to the spirit and custom of the department.

Yet, for all its virtues, the British Civil Service is becoming increasingly unpopular. Broadly the reason lies in the belief that the bureaucracy has become too powerful. As the role of government has extended over time, so arbitrary bureaucratic decisions have come to impinge ever more upon individuals who feel defenseless against the might of authority in the hands of the official who decides whether one is eligible for unemployment benefit or a supplementary pension, or to whom a municipal house for rent should be allocated. At the same time, civil servants are thought to have arrogated to themselves too much of the power that nominally resides with ministers. High and low, the influence of the civil servant has become pervasive in British society. And when British affairs have—as many observers feel—been conducted with obvious lack of success, it is inevitable that much of the blame will be attached to the professional group that has been involved in most of the decisions behind closed doors. A secretive governing caste, which is how the Civil Service is regarded by many British people, needs to run things pretty well if it is to be accepted.

There are nearly three quarters of a million people working in the Civil Service itself, pushing the paper and influencing the decisions of the central government of the United Kingdom. Over and above that figure, many thousands more work in the nationalized industries, public agencies, and local authorities. The public resentment against officialdom is directed against administrators in all these fields. Objections to the excessive power of civil servants in government, however, are focused upon a much smaller group—those who belong to what used to be the administrative grades of the service, which nowadays means in effect those of the rank of principal and above. Ranging upward there are 5,200 principals, 1,150 assistant secretaries, 575 under secretaries, 150 deputy secretaries, and 40 permanent secretaries. Of these it is only the under secretaries and above who consistently exercise significant influence. So for the purposes of assessing the power of the Civil Service, we are really thinking of fewer than 800 mandarins, nearly all of whom have spent their whole careers working their way up in the service.

In theory the role of the Civil Service is clear and limited. It is there to offer advice to ministers and to execute the wishes of ministers. Every decision within a department is taken in the name of its minister. Hence the doctrine of ministerial responsibility: it is the minister who must take the blame in public and in Parliament for any blunder, even when he has not committed it personally. This doctrine is wearing thin because it conflicts with what everybody knows to be the facts. How can it really be thought to be the fault of the minister when a junior civil servant in his department makes an error? No minister could conceivably supervise all the detailed work of a large department. The normal practice these days is for control of its executive operations to be left to the senior civil servants.[2]

The theory of ministerial responsibility fails to accord with current practice not only in placing an impossible requirement on a minister to supervise down the line, but also in expecting the mandarins to be remarkably self-effacing at the top. Critics do not believe that they are so self-effacing. It was of the senior mandarins that a recent report complained:

> There is a conflict between their superior intellect and the little that they have to offer in a practical way. There is, as should be, no role in our society for people with little to offer in a practical way but civil servants have got round this stumbling block by inventing a role for themselves. The role that they have invented for themselves is that of governing the country. They see themselves, to the detriment of democracy, as politicians writ large. And of course as politicians writ large they seek to govern the country according to their own narrow, well-defined interests, tastes, education and background, none of which fit them on the whole to govern a modern technological, industrialised, pluralist and urbanised society.[3]

A number of charges are mixed together in this extravagant assault: civil servants run the government themselves instead of allowing the democratically elected politicians to do so; they are biased by their social background; and they lack the professional skills for the job.

POWER OF THE CIVIL SERVICE

Are civil servants too powerful? The belief that a minister is easily programmed by his civil servants, who keep him in a comfortable cocoon where he is smoothly and efficiently served but cut off from most other sources of information, was fostered most notably by the posthumously published diaries of Richard Crossman, who served in the Wilson Labour Cabinet from 1964 to 1970.[4] Crossman was a witness of erratic judgment, and it would be unwise to accept all his evidence at face value. Some of it tells us more about his difficulties in handling civil servants than about their determination to dominate ministers. The belief that the Civil Service wields excessive power, however, does not rest upon Crossman's evidence alone.

It is natural that a minister who comes to office with years of political experience behind him but often no deep knowledge of his department's subject matter, should take particular account of advice from civil servants who have been dealing with it for years. Modern government has become so complex that in some areas even an experienced minister must depend upon specialists' advice. Only a genius or a fool would do otherwise—and public life in Britain, as in so many other countries, is rather short of geniuses these days. Moreover, the advice proffered to a minister often goes farther than the necessary tasks of filling in the gaps in his knowledge and providing a useful source of ideas. Individual departments, as we have said, often have their own policy line, irrespective of who forms the government of the day. There is also an unseen government machine that exists beneath the visible political government and in certain respects acts almost independently of it. Much of the work of government is done by cabinet committees, whose membership and even existence are not formally acknowledged to the public. These committees, which are normally composed of ministers from the different departments, whether of cabinet or junior rank, examine issues before they are brought to the Cabinet with a view to preparing an agreed recommendation—and are even empowered on some questions to make decisions on behalf of the Cabinet. Beneath each of these ministerial committees is a parallel committee of officials, where many of the deals are made between different departments. Ministers will then be briefed by the civil servants in accordance with the compromise the latter have worked out. So, provided the advice is accepted, the decision is effectively taken by civil servants even though formally it must be subsequently agreed to after debate in a ministerial committee. Once a week the permanent secretaries—the most senior civil servants of all departments—meet together to keep in touch with each other's thinking.

It is within this Civil Service labyrinth not only that many of the decisions of government are made but that the reputations of these officials are made and lost. This is one of the principal differences between the British and the American bureaucracies. In Washington an official within any agency of the executive branch who loses the confidence of Congress, especially of the relevant congressional committees, has suffered a damaging setback in his career. If his judgment is not taken seriously on Capitol Hill, he will be handicapped in his capacity to deliver his policies and will be of correspondingly less value to his agency.

In Britain, parliamentary support can for the most part be taken for granted; and where it cannot be, it is not much influenced by any civil servant. Unless a civil servant is very senior, he will not even be known to most M.P.'s. There is no dialogue of any consequence between parliamentarians and civil servants. An official may from time to time appear before a select committee, where he will be infinitely courteous, apparently deferential, perhaps condescending, and will try to keep out of trouble. This evasiveness may change as Parliament strengthens its new select committees; but a somewhat distant attitude toward Parliament is sustained by institutional practices that foster distance and is ingrained in most British officials.

William Rodgers, a former Labour Cabinet member, went so far as to say: "I am not sure that the Civil Service as a whole, and some younger civil servants in particular, fully appreciate that a minister's first duty is to Parliament and that Parliament is and should be, in the fullest sense, sovereign."[5] This lack of appreciation is reinforced by the knowledge that even a minister's approval is generally of less consequence to an official's career than is his standing among his Civil Service colleagues. If they do not trust his word or his judgment, in particular if he loses the confidence of the Treasury, then in future he will have the same difficulty in obtaining consent for departmental policies as has an American official who is out of favor on the Hill.

For these various reasons civil servants have from time to time been known to lean a little hard on their ministers. One of the most pernicious tactics is the manipulation of deadlines. Papers are sometimes submitted to ministers at the last minute asking for a swift decision, perhaps overnight, as a matter of necessity, with the purpose of forcing compliance out of a minister at pistol point. There have also been occasions when a private company has tried the same technique on civil servants, and there is a chain reaction. A company will inform the Department of Industry that it must receive government help immediately or face catastrophe. The department thrusts the request on the Treasury, which in turn thrusts it on ministers. There are also instances where last-minute drafts of important public papers are offered to ministers when there will be the greatest difficulty in amending them if the embarrassment of postponed publication is to be avoided.

There is also the technique of foot-dragging. For example, not long ago one minister wrote to another asking for certain information. After about a fortnight a reply was sent at official level, but the receiving official did not send it up to his minister until after a further delay and then only as the result of a specific request. This was a case not of outright opposition but of quietly trying to withold information because the line of questioning suggested an unwelcome trend in policy.

151

There have been other instances of bureaucratic game playing with ministers. Tony Benn, who served in both the Wilson and the Callaghan cabinets and is one of the leading Labour left-wingers, gave some specific examples in a television program where he strongly attacked the Civil Service.[6]

One example was of a leak at the nuclear power plant at Windscale in 1976, just at the time it was proposed to enlarge Windscale so that it could handle radioactive waste from Japan. Mr. Benn was then Secretary of State for Energy, but the first he heard of the leak was in the newspapers; he suspected that the information had been kept from him by his officials because they were afraid it would affect his judgment in the Cabinet on the enlargement of Windscale, which they advocated. Another instance Mr. Benn gave was of a contract in 1970 for the British nuclear industry to obtain uranium from Namibia—a contract that was approved by officials from the Department of Energy without informing the Cabinet, even though the government had said that it wished to be consulted before any uranium contract was signed.[7]

It is not only in relation to national policy, though, that the Civil Service is believed to exercise its power. One reason for its current unpopularity is that it is thought to do so in its own interests. One must be careful not to describe the Civil Service as a monolith in its working operations. There are intense rivalries between one department and another behind the closed doors of Whitehall, the street on which most of the major ministries are located. To some extent these rivalries are healthy, because conflict ensures a searching scrutiny of programs and policies and a thorough consideration of alternatives. It would be better if the struggle between departments more often took the form of a rigorous examination of options: the coinage of debate is in practice usually somewhat debased; and there have been a good many instances where the public interest has suffered because of the inability of departments to cooperate with each other. But it is not realistic to expect government anywhere to be conducted in the style of an academic seminar: struggle over power is a persistent feature of the process of government; and there is no major capital in the world where there is no rivalry between the principal institutions of government.

When the interest of the service as a whole is at issue, however, there is a closing of the ranks. Successive ministers have, for example, felt that the service has been less than fully cooperative when asked to make cuts in its own staff. There is also much public dissatisfaction at the extremely favorable terms it has secured for itself over pensions, which are linked to the retail price index so as to protect retired civil servants from the ravages of inflation. This principle was enshrined by act of Parliament in 1971. To be fair, this advantage is not confined to the Civil Service. It applies to all in public employment, including a good many low-paid workers. Nonetheless, these conditions are regarded with envy by those working in the private sector, hardly any of whom are similarly protected.[8]

POLITICAL BIASES OF THE CIVIL SERVICE

All these aspects of Civil Service power apply whichever party is in office. The accusation is often heard that officials are more biased against a Labour government because of their social background. It has been the experience of all Labour administrations since Attlee was last Prime Minister in 1951 that they have proved to be less radical in office than they promised (or threatened) to be while they were in opposition. A gulf has consequently opened between Labour ministers and many of their supporters. Some ex-ministers who look for an alibi to explain their relative caution find it in the Civil Service: "We were stopped from doing what we wanted to" is the lament.

Not all former Labour ministers take this line, however. Mr. Rodgers has declared: "I look back on almost all my eleven years of government as happy ones. During this time I came to respect the great majority of the civil servants with whom I had to deal and to regard some with real affection. With few exceptions, they were able, hardworking and loyal."[9] This statement suggests that there is little substance in the charge of outright party bias. If such a thing existed, the sharp-eyed Mr. Rodgers would have noticed. No doubt some individuals in the Civil Service are biased, but as a whole the service takes pride in its political impartiality and its ability to serve governments of any complexion. In certain respects Labour policy must have particular attractions for officials. A party that believes in active government is more likely to favor bureaucratic solutions: certainly it is more likely to end up with a powerful bureaucracy whatever it may think it is doing. It was a former Labour minister (Douglas Jay) who coined the phrase, "The gentleman in Whitehall knows best."

When the Thatcher government took office in May 1979, there were many misgivings in Whitehall. The Conservative rejection of an incomes policy, the insistence on more industrial relations legislation, the demand for severe public expenditure cuts, the emphasis upon controlling the money supply as a means of curbing inflation, and the generally abrasive style of the new administration—all either cut across existing departmental policy preferences or implied a disturbingly sharp rate of change. The Treasury, by far the most powerful of all the home departments, appeared to be less at ease with its Conservative team of ministers than with any recent administration—not so much because it opposed government policies as because it lacked the conviction of the ministers that the new policies would work. A world-weary pessimism may have overtaken the officials, but this is quite different from party bias in any direction.

As a matter of course, civil servants subject the policies of an incoming government to searching scrutiny so that ministers can be aware of all practical difficulties before implementing a particular commitment. This scrutiny can be an uncomfortable experience for a newly appointed minister if the policy in question has not been thought through adequately in opposition—as is often the case with incoming governments in Britain as elsewhere, and particularly with Labour governments because the party does not have the resources for an adequate research operation in opposition. Nonetheless, disconcerting though it may be, it is a necessary function for officials to warn ministers in advance of the pitfalls in any course of action.

There is less justification for the extreme caution that characterizes much Civil Service thinking. This caution may be mistaken for political bias because it is often more slow-moving than politicians believe is warranted by circumstances. There are a number of reasons for caution. Adventurous spirits are usually not attracted by a lifelong career in a bureaucracy, even in such a powerful one as Britain's. Moreover, the system is one that penalizes failure rather than rewards success. Even though the doctrine of ministerial responsibility has in practice been modified, one of the cardinal sins for a civil servant is to land his minister in an embarrassing position. An action that leads to awkward questioning of the minister in Parliament can be a blot on a civil servant's record; a public scandal is catastrophe for the ambitious, though dismissal is a rare fate for a civil servant. A successful initiative is likely to be much less widely noticed. The minister will probably grab the credit in public; a good idea may well not catch his attention until it becomes quite widely supported within the department; and, in any case, it is usually easier to pick out an administrative error than to be sure what is good advice.

In the British government, where so much takes place behind closed doors, there is little opportunity for a civil servant to become publicly associated with policy. Furthermore, where there is little career movement, there is little personal need to establish a reputation with a wider public. It often makes sense, therefore, for the British bureaucrat to play safe. The British system encourages civil servants to cover their tracks, to divide responsibility, to arrange always to have consulted as many people as possible. There are thus endless meetings, and responsibility can never quite be pinned to one individual, if that individual is smart enough to avoid it.

155

POLITICAL VALUES

So although civil servants do bring pressure to bear upon ministers in one way or another, they are not constantly seeking to foist upon reluctant ministers a civil service blueprint for running the country. The reality is much less clear-cut. There are established lines of departmental thinking; but, for all the intellectual ability at its command, the Civil Service is not a hothouse of bold ideas. Much of its influence is skeptical, if not negative. Where it is not skeptical, some ministers complain, it tends to tell ministers what it thinks they want to hear—another, though rather different, example of the pervasive caution. This is one of the principal reasons that the system needs to be opened up—a point that we shall elaborate later in this chapter.

SOCIAL BACKGROUND

Even if there is no significant deliberate bias, may there not be unconscious bias as a result of educational and social background? That is a separate and more difficult question. The Expenditure Committee Report on the Civil Service found that, in the five years from 1971 to 1975, 50 percent of recruits were Oxford or Cambridge graduates even though they amounted to only 21.6 percent of applicants.[10] There was also some evidence of a bias—in a statistical sense—in favor of former pupils from independent schools. In 1973–75, 29.2 percent of applicants from Oxford or Cambridge had gone to fee-paying schools, but 34.6 percent of Oxbridge recruits into the service in those years were graduates from these schools. The entry from other universities showed that while ex-independent school pupils accounted for only 8.6 percent of the applicants, they won 21.3 percent of the places.

Such figures must be interpreted with care. They may reveal more about the British educational system than about the Civil Service. So long as a high proportion of the most able students go to Oxford or Cambridge—as they still unquestionably do, even if not to the same extent as in previous generations—this proportion is bound to be reflected in any method of selection for the Civil Service that is based upon merit.[11] A massive attempt to redress the balance would actually lead to a decline in the caliber of recruits.

The advantage apparently possessed by ex-independent school pupils may be partly explained in the same way: they are in general the children of relatively successful parents who have been eager for them to do well at school and university. Parental stimulus has been shown to be an important factor in educational performance, but it is not the only factor. The comparative success of pupils from these schools does suggest that the Civil Service has a preference for the articulate, who may not be the most profound. The assured young man from a good social background is most likely to shine in the interviews and group discussions that form an important part of the selection procedure. There is not necessarily deliberate social bias, but such a system must favor the quick person with a safe comment rather than the one who hesitantly expresses more original ideas.

It would be a mistake, though, to make too much of the social background of civil servants. There is no monopoly of access for Oxford or Cambridge graduates from independent schools. Many recruits come from state schools and other universities. Moreover, the spirit and the style of the service are so strong that a few years of membership in the caste of civil servants tends to mold recruits more thoroughly in their ways than the school and university from which they came.

POLITICAL VALUES

TRAINING FOR THE CIVIL SERVICE

More disturbing than the influence of social background is the lack of specialists within the service.

There is disagreement about how far this lack is a matter of preference in selection. There is no doubt that arts graduates stand a relatively better chance than scientists. The Expenditure Committee found that, from 1971 to 1975, 56.7 percent of recruits were arts and humanities graduates even though they amounted to only 42.5 percent of applicants. That imbalance may have been a reflection of bias on the part of the selectors; it may also have been that the scientists were on average simply not such good candidates. The committee said that they had

> some reason to believe that the best qualified scientists do not apply to become administration trainees in as high numbers as the best qualified arts graduates. This may well be because they prefer to work as scientists whilst in their twenties when scientists are reputed to do their best work as such. A scientist may prefer to work in those leading industrial companies where, after he has done scientific work, he has a ready chance of promotion to administrative work.[12]

It is understandable, and not at all contrary to the national interest, if the best scientists prefer to go into industry rather than into government service. There would be more to worry about if many scientists were going into the Civil Service. If some of those who do offer themselves are of lower quality than the arts graduates they are competing against, then there can be no valid complaint if they are not chosen. An inferior scientist would not necessarily make a better administrator. If differences in the quality of applicants are the sole explanation for the mix of disciplines in recruitment, then it is a perfectly good one.

It is hard to believe, though, that this is really the whole story. The tradition of the service fashioned by the Northcote-Trevelyan reforms of 1855 has always favored the generalist, the person who

158

could turn his hand to any task and whose skill lay in what was held to be judgment and capacity to administer rather than in any technical accomplishment. This tradition may seem just another example of the well-known British preference for the amateur over the professional, but there is more to it than that. Generalist capacities may in fact be needed. Mr. Rodgers has said that "as a minister, faced with the need for advice and, hopefully, some understanding of the political and governmental process, generalist ability—and a capacity to learn—is what I require of the officials that surround me."[13]

Coming from a former Labour minister, this testimony is not to be ignored. It is certainly true that a senior adviser with little political or social understanding is a disaster, whether he be a scientist or a classicist. Yet the role of government has so expanded that today there are many tasks for which a broad common sense is simply not enough. That was the belief of the Fulton Committee on the Civil Service, whose principal conclusion in 1968 was that the service was "still too much based on the philosophy of the amateur (or 'generalist' or 'all-rounder')."[14] The report—which was the product of the most comprehensive recent study of the service, even though its findings have remained highly controversial—went on to advocate that "the service should develop greater professionalism both among specialists (e.g. scientists and engineers) and administrators." It explained that "for the former this means more training in management, and opportunities for greater responsibility and wider careers. For the latter it means enabling them to specialise in particular areas of government." Neither recommendation has been properly applied.

It is inevitable these days that governments, and consequently their civil servants, are widely involved in commercial activities— sometimes conducting them, more often supervising or monitoring the work of others. Britain has a large public sector, and each of the nationalized industries is responsible to some minister or other. In the private sector there is so much government money given to industry in loans and grants, and so much government regulation of industrial activities, that officials have a role to play there as well. This remains true even under an administration like Mrs. Thatcher's that believes as a point of doctrine that government should withdraw as far as possible from such concerns.

The conduct of economic enterprise is not an area for which British civil servants are well equipped. Sometimes their failings are revealed for all to see. There was the case in 1964, for example, when Ferranti Ltd., the electronics company, made a large refund to public funds after making an exceptionally large profit from a guided missiles contract with the former Ministry of Aviation. The ministry itself concluded that the contractor had taken advantage of its ignorance. Whether the company was at fault is another matter: what was beyond dispute was that the civil servants concerned lacked the technical knowledge to estimate costs with sufficient accuracy to draw up a prudent contract.[15]

During the 1960s and early 1970s the Crown Agents, whose principal function is to provide financial services to overseas governments and other public bodies, ran up losses of over £200 million through unsuccessful speculation in the property market and had to seek a loan from the British government.[16] There have been other less dramatic instances of officials finding themselves lacking in expertise. Whatever the advantages of the generalist tradition, there are some tasks in government today that require more than general judgment and a readiness to learn on the job.

It is not just expertise in particular fields that the Civil Service lacks. The experience of its members is too narrow. Nearly all those in what was the administrative class—the mandarins and the potential mandarins of principal level and above—join the Civil Service immediately after university and stay on until retirement. There is a scheme for late entry, which provides for an intake of about twenty to twenty-five recruits a year, whose average age is usually about forty. Something like forty specialists enter the service each year after the usual age—aside from inspectors of schools who are a special category. But these are limited exceptions to the general rule, which is that the regular Civil Service is a lifetime career offering no experience in commerce, industry, finance, or, indeed, in any other walk of life.

SECRECY IN GOVERNMENT

It is hardly surprising that such an enclosed service is secretive in its working practices. There is no Freedom of Information Act in Britain as there is in the United States and some Scandinavian countries. Rather than encouraging open government, the law in Britain operates in precisely the opposite direction. The notorious Section 2 of the Official Secrets Act of 1911, which is still on the statute book, makes it a criminal offense to pass on or to receive any confidential sketch, plan, model, article, note, document, or information obtained by a person holding office under the Crown. The item concerned does not even have to be important.

The one consoling feature of this catch-all section is that it is so absurdly restrictive that it can hardly ever be enforced. To enforce it literally would be out of the question, and to enforce it at all is difficult because it is so widely ridiculed. For that reason the Thatcher government decided shortly after taking office to replace it with a limited measure that would narrow the area of restriction but provide a more feasible basis for prosecution. Although this measure was presented as a piece of liberalizing legislation, its effect would have been precisely the opposite. Under its terms, for example, a newspaper could have been prosecuted for revealing any abuse in the operation of the security services—and ran a greater risk that prosecutions would actually have been brought. The measure was described as a rapier replacing a blunderbuss and was vigorously attacked in the press. Fortunately the government took the opportunity of the furor over the Anthony Blunt spy case to withdraw the bill on the grounds that it would have prevented the exposure of Blunt. Thus a bad situation was not made worse, but it still leaves Britain with an unreasonably restrictive law.

It is sometimes argued that since the law cannot be applied, it does not matter; but in fact it reinforces the administrative pressures toward secrecy. Politicians and civil servants who might otherwise be somewhat open are deterred by having signed the Official Secrets Act—and thus exposed themselves to the admittedly distant threat of prosecution for disclosing information that might embarrass the government but certainly not endanger the state.

OPENING UP GOVERNMENT

Some serious attempts have been made in recent years to open up the workings of government. The practice was started in 1967 of publishing occasional "green papers," which would be discussion documents on particular topics, possibly setting out alternative courses, but without in any sense committing the government to any line of action. These are by way of contrast to the familiar white papers, which set out government intentions without having any force of law. Green papers have been a useful development because they provide the requisite opportunity for greater public scrutiny of options before the government is committed to any one of them. In this way the potential weaknesses of a policy can be exposed before the government has gone so far that it cannot abandon it without public humiliation. It would be wrong to claim this as more than a marginal advance, however, because green papers are still heavily outnumbered by white ones.

In 1977 another potentially valuable initiative was taken when the then head of the Home Civil Service, Sir Douglas Allen, now Lord Croham, wrote to all heads of departments with the express approval of the Prime Minister asking that in the preparation of policy studies the background material should so far as possible be kept separate from the advice tendered to ministers, so that this information could then more easily be published. More frequent publication of such material would indeed be valuable, but this directive has been largely ignored. It ought to be revived and applied in the spirit as well as in the letter.

The best way to open up government, however, is to make it in the interests of civil servants to do so. If there were in Parliament strong select committees which could amend legislation and influence the allocation of public money, departments would soon find it advantageous to disclose information to them. Such bodies are small enough to have a serious dialogue with departments, and they would then be powerful enough to make it worth the while of busy ministers and overburdened civil servants to take the trouble to see that they were fully informed. Their active approval would be worth having, and it would be best secured by a full presentation not just of hard facts but of the reasons that a particular policy had been preferred to other options. It is because congressional committees are powerful that there is competitive leaking of information by departments and agencies in Washington—because Washington bureaucrats have been convinced of their civic duty to open government; but because they know that public discussion can be a means of persuading other political actors to help get their policies adopted. It is not enough for bureaucrats to win the arguments within the executive branch.

A strengthened Parliament would also be one of the best correctives to the excessive power of the Civil Service. Whether it is excessive, Civil Service power is not accumulated through evil motives. It comes rather from the circumstances in which the service operates. Even Mr. Benn, one of the most critical of former ministers, has said that "if a minister is determined in the handling of his own departmental matters, and if he knows, he can insist upon a decision."[17] The trouble is that all too often a minister does not know enough to insist. He does not have alternative advice at his disposal; and once he has taken his decision on the basis of Civil Service advice, he will find himself overruled by Parliament only in exceptional instances.

163

If a minister knew that his decision would be subjected to rigorous scrutiny in a select committee before it was approved, he would be more likely to insist upon taking alternative advice in advance. Even if he did not, the committee would do so before allowing the policy to be implemented.

The need is not so much for internal reforms designed to weaken the Civil Service. At the moment Britain has a civil service of considerable intellectual qualities and a number of weaknesses. If the service was to be emasculated, morale would probably be lowered, and inferior talent attracted; the outcome would be a service with different but no fewer weaknesses. The better course would be to open up the system of advising the political decision makers. One means to this end would be to deprive the Civil Service of its virtual monopoly of advice, to make it compete on more equal terms with other sources of analysis and ideas.

A strong select committee system would tend to have that effect; because, in the interests of building their own competence and power, committees would insist upon having their own advisers of high quality, who would tend to balance the influence of the Civil Service.[18] This would be all the more likely to happen if Britain had a few "think tanks" of the same caliber as those in the United States. There are a number of such establishments in London—the Royal Institute of International Affairs (Chatham House); the International Institute of Strategic Studies; the Policy Studies Institute, bringing together the former Political and Economic Planning (PEP) and the Centre for Studies in Social Policy; the National Institution for Economic and Social Research; the Outer Circle Policy Group; and the Trade Policy Research Centre—to name some of the principal ones. Although they do much useful work, they are neither large enough nor command sufficient resources for the broader purpose of challenging or even supplementing Civil Service advice consistently over a wide area.

There was the idea a little while ago of establishing a "British Brookings," a broadly based policy studies institute on the model of the Brookings Institution in Washington, but that proposal fell through for a variety of reasons. What is required is not a single organization that would form some kind of alternative civil service, but a number of bodies each of which would be sufficiently substantial to make a contribution of consequence to the pool of ideas on which public policy could be based. A few really strong think tanks of this sort could both conduct studies on which select committees could regularly draw—and on which select committees could rely because of their established reputation—and second staff to serve the select committees directly. It is not that British think tanks do not do any of these things now; it is that they are not big enough, and generally do not cover a sufficiently broad field, to command the influence they should.

There should also be a broader range of experience available to advise ministers from within the Civil Service. This experience could be achieved in two ways. In the first place, career officials could more frequently be seconded elsewhere for a period. They could become special assistants to members of Parliament, as Mr. Rodgers suggests; or more probably they could act as advisers to select committees—as committees in the Norwegian parliament, the *Storting,* are served. These officials could have tours of duty in local government, industry, or commerce.

Secondly, there could be more flexible arrangements for entry into the service. In the culture of London there is no chance of encouraging the in-and-outer to play the role that he does in Washington. British career structures require people much more than is necessary in the United States to get on a single ladder and keep climbing it. Nonetheless, a few notable people have managed to combine important work in both public and private sectors to a significant degree. It would be possible to have more temporary civil servants and more latecomers to the service. The practice for ministers occasionally to have advisers from outside the service has existed for many years. The Wilson Labour government of 1964–70 extended the practice considerably and can be regarded as having originated the present system of special advisers. In the Heath Conservative government of 1970–74, six or seven ministers had special assistants paid from party funds. Then in the Wilson Labour government that took office in 1974, the practice was put on a more systematic basis, each minister being allowed up to two special assistants paid from public funds. By the time the Labour government left office, there were twenty-six such assistants. They performed three functions: they provided specialized advice from the standpoint of someone politically committed to the government's program; they could offer political counsel and alert a minister, in a way that an established civil servant could not, to the political implications of proposals coming before the Cabinet and cabinet committees from other departments; and they could be a link with the party in the country, with which busy ministers can so easily lose touch.[19]

Unfortunately the Thatcher government has adopted a much more restrictive attitude toward special advisers, with no minister being allowed to have more than one. Only fourteen of them have been appointed to be paid by public funds, though a few more are paid out of Conservative party funds. One difficulty is that under British conditions it has not proved easy to get enough people of the necessary caliber to take on a job whose influence is uncertain and whose career prospects are negligible. Most of the best have been people of established authority in their field, often from academic life. Many of the others have been aspiring politicians, whose capacity in the job has varied a great deal. It would be easier to recruit good special advisers if there were strong policy research centers, which could be a useful source of recruits and offer an assurance of future employment for the former special adviser who might otherwise have difficulty resuming his previous career. Ideally, each cabinet minister should have up to four or five special advisers, who would not have any regular administrative functions within the department. Administration would be left in the hands of the senior career officials, to whom the special advisers should be a stimulus and a challenge.

More latecomers to the Civil Service itself should also be encouraged: the person who is experienced in other employment is an asset. This advantage was demonstrated during the Second World War when many people entered the service from other walks of life —most of them only for the duration of the war, some permanently. This was an exceptional period when there was a significant flow into the Civil Service from academic life. John Maynard Keynes, for example, was an immensely successful temporary civil servant in both world wars. The firm preference in normal times for an established service to which employees devote their whole careers is in keeping with the general British approach to careers. It also represents a preference for integrity over vitality.

The integrity of the British Civil Service is to a degree safeguarded by its exclusive nature. This integrity is epitomized by the rule that no senior official may, without permission, take a job, within two years of leaving the service, with an employer who has any business relationships with the government. In practice, however, permission is usually given when sought. With more latecomers into the service, it would be natural to expect a greater movement in mid-career in the other direction—a trend that is already increasing.[20] There would be a risk of corruption if the two-way flow were increased between industry and the Civil Service. There are, however, greater risks than this—of ignorance and of incapacity to devise and execute intelligent policy—in keeping a monopoly of the administration of public business in the hands of a relatively insular caste.

We are struck with the extent to which many innovations, proposed or actually in motion in contemporary British government, add up to attempts to break this monopoly and to diversify the sources of policy planning and evaluation. By at least one interpretation, a major effect of strengthening parliamentary committees would be to increase public knowledge and political discussion on alternative courses of action open to the government. The persistence of demands for an increased capability in the private sector to do policy studies of all sorts amounts to a proposal for better knowledge of the main problems being grappled with in the middle ranges of the bureaucracies, and for the availability of second and third opinions, based on original analysis, about the solutions fixed upon by civil servants. Political advisers, following career paths of their own, are expected primarily to expand ministers' knowledge of the latest developments beyond the range normally undertaken by their departments—into party politics and into matters that come to the ministers by virtue of their position in the Cabinet and on which the ministers' own departments have no firm position, for two examples. They would also, however, be expected from time to time to feed back advice to ministers that would have an impact on decision making. This expectation is undoubtedly the main reason for resistance to political advisers on the part of civil servants. The more far-sighted and able public administrators, however, do not doubt that their work could withstand scrutiny, and welcome the added breadth of perspective that political advisers bring to departmental decision making. Here, as elsewhere, it is the natural prejudices of conservative institutions and their loyal defenders, more than the fruits of experience, that have held back the establishment of political advisers on a secure and regular basis.

Even the now-aborted drive toward devolution can be seen as an attempt to create institutions—assemblies—positioned so as to be able to lobby public administrators into changing their ways toward regions having unique identities and consequently special needs.

None of these various attempts to leaven and modify the processes of public administration in Great Britain are guaranteed to increase the effectiveness of public policy. All, however, have the potential of increasing general understanding of the premises upon which policy is based, and of explicitly testing these premises against the desires of a wide range of groups and through reference to known or ascertainable facts. Well-run societies with democratic values may not always be free of mistaken public policy, but responsibility for mistakes—as for successes—must be widely shared as a means of increasing the legitimacy of government among those who bear its costs and reap its benefits.

PART III

INSTEAD OF A

CONCLUSION

Britain's three overwhelming problems—reduced economic productivity, social solidarity, and world influence—have interacted to sap the confidence of its leadership. The restoration of leadership depends, we believe, on the strengthening of British political institutions by broadening their capacities to build public consensus and to allow differently situated élites—Parliament and government, civil servants and outside policy analysts—to learn from one another. Other, more deeply rooted political resources also exist in Great Britain, although not all have been sufficiently developed. Even so, not all the contradictions of British life, in their splendid variety, are tractable to measures that British leaders are likely to be willing to employ. This, we suggest, is less important than the recovery of confidence among leaders and citizens alike, and a willingness to apply the resources at hand to the tasks of rebuilding British prosperity and hence sustain the capacity to make the choices that will preserve and extend a unique way of life.

CHAPTER 7

The Recovery of Confidence

Books generally come to an end before the problems they describe. The great civilization that has been created in the British Isles has already outlived countless obituary notices. These are two good reasons for concluding on an inconclusive note. A third is that muddling through is a British invention that makes it uncommonly difficult for even the most careful observers to tell on whose side the forces of reason and organization, or those of inertia and entropy are playing, never mind which of these forces is winning.

Consider some of the following problems: The British pride themselves on maintaining a constitutional structure in which properly constituted governments in Parliament can with a majority vote do far-reaching things, without being held back by the reservations of intransigent minority interests. This structure is frequently accounted a good thing, since it prevents immobilism; but it also means that a succeeding government can with facility undo what one government has done. The bracing lack of systemic checks and balances can, in the event of sharp divisions on policy and only modestly oscillating majorities in succeeding elections, make for great difficulties in the economic planning of the private sector. Possibly the most conspicuous example was the nationalization of steel by the Labour government in 1951, the denationalization in 1953 by a Conservative government, and renationalization in 1967 by the Wilson government.

A policy machine that goes full speed ahead with occasional screeching stops can be observed to create a turbulent environment for investors, managers, and unions. It can be especially difficult for private sector firms that are likely candidates for nationalization, or renationalization, to attract the private capital they need to compete successfully. The net effect of Britain's smoothly working constitutional machinery may be to create a heavy economic burden on the state.

This is only one of the complaints that are raised by critics of the British constitution. Governments that enjoy parliamentary majorities may not enjoy majority support among British voters, yet may act with all the lack of restraint of those governments that have such support. This situation leads some critics to demand changes in the electoral system, which presently elects members of Parliament in single-member districts by plurality vote—a system known as "first-past-the-post." Proportional voting would correct that, but it is not favored by the major parties and is hence an unlikely eventuality. It would be one way of introducing some of the immobility that the unwritten British constitution pointedly avoids. Other critics, as we have mentioned, have suggested that citizens should have enumerated rights that only special majorities could disturb; and some have gone so far as to propose the strengthening of parliamentary oversight over the government—a measure that we ourselves favor because we do not fear the occasional frustration of purposeful government. Traditionalists may well cherish more than we do the illusions of popular accountability, decisiveness in policy making, and political responsibility which come along with governments that are constitutionally entirely free to act.

Like all observers of contemporary Britain, we have remarked upon the ways in which British localism, parochialism, resistance to innovation, and disinclination to hustle make for a culture that is geared to low productivity. There is another side to this picture. British steadiness of habit, loyalty to locale, to family, and even to class norms—indeed to social boundaries of all sorts—has bred by international standards an unusually law-abiding and civil people. Like any big city, London has its crime—petty and otherwise; but perhaps only in London among big cities of the Western world is it possible to see flimsily secured bicycles parked in the middle of town, and windowboxes on front stoops, unmolested from one year to the next. The British respect their laws and themselves; their ordinary policemen still walk about unarmed.

Homicide rates in Britain are remarkably low by American standards: 1600 killings versus 21,000 in one recent year. Corrected for disparities in population size, Britain comes up roughly 14,000 murders short of the United States annually.[1] Or consider the toll from traffic accidents: Britain's miserable and crowded road system produces far fewer accidents per mile than the world norm. Authorities fall back on the lame, but undoubtedly correct, explanation that, unlike all other civilized peoples, Britons retain their courteous habits even when behind the wheel of an auto.[2] When afoot they spontaneously form up into queues, even in this day and age. Peace and order are no mean virtues in a civic culture, especially when they are maintained as voluntary contributions by the citizenry to their common life—rather than, as in so many places the world around, by armies, secret police, and other instruments of state repression.

We wonder, as so many have wondered before us, how much British civic decency is at risk if cultural patterns change sufficiently to promote higher productivity. Yet civil decency may also be put at risk if there is no economic growth, if the different sectors of British society compete more intensely over the division of a static national income. Unlike many observers, particularly foreigners who are a little too overjoyed by the stubborn British propensity for quaintness, we believe Britain must make the effort

173

and invest in higher productivity. Even quaintness is expensive in the modern world, and tourists can defray only a part of the bill.

Or we have the paradox of a brilliantly trained civil service, surely one of the wonders of the world, recruited from the best that British higher education has to offer, and given real and meaningful responsibility, yet unable to find solutions to big central problems with which it must cope—such as maintaining an economy that produces an adequate standard of living in the face of rapid technological change. Whatever Britain lacks, it is clearly not brains in the public sector. Is it possible that brains are not enough? Or perhaps it is the public sector that is not enough.

Nobody seriously doubts that something has to be done to revive both sides of the private sector—management and labor alike. This necessity, curiously enough, cuts athwart settled norms of the British status system; shrewd observers suggest that status as well as monetary incentives will have to be supplied to entrepreneurs, and that both high status as well as an intellectually sophisticated advanced education will be needed to lure Britons into business. A generation ago Harold Laski lamented that there was nothing in Britain quite like the Harvard Law School to provide intellectual leadership to the bench and bar.[3] Far more might he complain of the contemporary lack of a British counterpart to the Harvard Business School.

Yet, in international trade and finance, in banking and insurance, the city of London is second to none. Clearly the spirit is willing, but the social organization is weak. The gross statistics over the long run on days lost to strikes do not bear out the common perception of a bloody-minded labor force. The statistics on productivity do, however, bear out the common perception of an unproductive labor force. There are many examples of overmanning, featherbedding, immobility, and excessive traditionalism in the labor force—symptoms of acute anxiety about the capacity of the society as a whole to finance a transition to industrial modernity without excessively burdening working people and their families. We think some of these anxieties are justified, and that entrepreneurs and economic planners will, whenever possible, have to bribe their way into the good graces of obsolete members of the British labor force, in part by retraining, in part through various sorts of golden handshakes. We do not know how frequently these strategies will be economically feasible; but we are convinced that they should be pursued, and that the countervailing desire of union bureaucrats to perpetuate their jurisdictions a generation after the end of any economic justification for the maintenance of jobs in a particular category ought not to be gratified. Such traditionalism invites ruin.

Paradoxes, anomalies, anachronisms, and contradictions living side by side are signs of complexity in a society, signs moreover that there is no overriding authority busily ironing out the wrinkles and enforcing a conformity in the patterns of reward that give meaning to diverse lives. In considering Britain's decline in the world, it is worth remembering that the liberal values of privacy and civility, the freedoms for individuals to think and write, to advocate and organize, and to move about unmolested are still the essence of a decent society; and these are still, by and large, values Great Britain upholds and protects to a degree that even more prosperous societies can properly envy.

It is worth remembering also that the decline of Great Britain is measured in relative, not absolute terms; that Britain is now a middling country in resources and in economic capabilities when ranged against its larger and more resourceful contemporaries, but nevertheless is richer, healthier, and better fed than the Britain of twenty, fifty, or one hundred years ago. So the economic costs of recent historical change, while they have been borne disproportionately by inhabitants of the British Isles, have nevertheless been deducted from an expanding national product and have curtailed the expansion of opportunity rather than the capacity of the British to take care of their own.

Even so, it is to the regeneration of opportunities that those who care about Britain's future must look, and hence to clusters of public choices that are at one and the same time economic and psychological in their import. What to do with the economic dividend, of a decade or two's duration, granted by the development of North Sea oil? Ideally the bulk of it should be spent in upgrading industry and in easing the movement of the labor force out of nonproductive activity. How can the labor force be persuaded to respond more positively in the face of social and economic change? Will it be possible to stimulate private sector investment by manipulation of the tax code? There is also the long-range problem of increasing incentives for the vocation of entrepreneur, of convincing Britons that a part of their future lies in successful participation in world markets, not as traders and bankers alone, but as producers as well.[4] Britain, always a leader in the study of the basic sciences, must lead as well in education for careers in technology, engineering, and marketing.

Throughout this book we have been describing a nation in decline with all the lack of confidence to be expected of a country in that condition. As we see it, this—far more than the economic malaise—is the central problem; or, rather, it is a prime cause of economic failure. A sense of pessimism has become pervasive in Britain today. It cripples the will to innovate. It affects the bureaucracy, whose institutional strength has often become an impediment to action, not because officials are disloyal, but because they have ceased to believe that anything will work. It inhibits parliamentary reform where it has bred caution over half-measures. It has its impact on the political parties struggling to redefine the terms of political debate so as to make them more relevant to current conditions. It prevents Britain from exercising the influence in the world that, even in its reduced circumstances, is still available to it.

It might be said that a preference for immobilism and stability has always been a feature of British society. That, however, is to accept the tourist's-eye view of Britain, a land of ancient castles, country churchyards, and horse guards on parade. The reality has been different. In the Victorian era, when British industry led the world and British power overseas was wielded with little inhibition, there was an acceptance, even an eagerness for change, and an expectation that change would be for the better which was sustained by the stability of British society. British experience then upheld the principle that only a confident country would have the will to innovate successfully over a period of time and to accept the strains of innovation. The aggressive, risk-taking entrepreneur was a dominant figure of that age.[5] Not only did Britain lead the way in the Industrial Revolution; there was also enough social stability to withstand the pressures of the Luddites and the Chartists without social revolution.

In the days, not all that long ago, when Britain was regarded as an example of a successful society, it was often claimed that the flexibility of the class system had safeguarded Britain from the social revolutions of continental Europe. Only in a country where there was perceptible, even if not rapid, movement up and down, would there be the preoccupation with class that has so astonished foreign observers. Indeed, the distinctive feature of British society in the past has been a preference for gradual change on the basis of national confidence.

That confidence is what has gone. Yet only when confidence returns will trade unions be prepared to change working practices so as to promote profits and to maximize the real living standards of their members, rather than simply to defend the jobs they have; and only then will employers be willing to invest in the belief that expansion will be profitable, or politicians and bureaucrats to adjust their practices to meet contemporary needs.

We do not claim to have a remedy for the restoration of confidence in Britain. The decline in confidence is no doubt a natural consequence of the nation's fall from a position in the world that it could not hope to have maintained; but the decline has gone farther than necessary and has diminished Britain's standing still more. What we have done is to indicate some of the areas where change could most profitably be achieved with a return of confidence and to assert our belief

177

that many of the difficulties that now look so daunting are susceptible to a revival of spirit.

"Where there is no hope," said Samuel Johnson, "there is no endeavor." The question for Britain is whether it will recover its readiness to hope and to renew constructive endeavor, or whether the pride that it retains will come only from contemplation of the past.

NOTES

Chapter 1

1. From 1950 to 1966 the per capita national income in Britain increased 37 percent. Another good index of prosperity, the number of telephones in use per 1,000 population, rose from 63.8 in 1937 to 86.9 in 1946, to 181.0 in 1965, to 267 in 1970.
2. The following table gives average annual growth rate for the GNPs of the major industrial nations.

Country	1950–65	1960–70	1970–75
Japan	8.8	10.5	6.8
Canada	4.4	5.6	4.8
France	4.6	5.7	3.9
Italy	5.4	5.3	3.8
United States	3.7	4.3	2.5
United Kingdom	2.9	2.9	2.3
West Germany	6.6	4.6	2.2

SOURCES: United Nations, *1976 Statistical Yearbook* (New York, 1977), pp. 676–79; and Charles Lewis Taylor and Michael C. Hudson, *World Handbook of Political and Social Indicators* (New Haven: Yale University Press, 1972), p. 306.

3. A convenient summary of these and other indicators is contained in Herbert Stein's essay "What Margaret Thatcher Knows," *The AEI Economist* (Washington, D.C.: The American Enterprise Institute, August 1979).
4. Recent figures on unionization of the work force show:

Trade Union Members as a Percentage of All Employees

Year	Italy	United Kingdom	West Germany	Nether-lands	France	United States
1960	55–60%	43%	38%	38%	24%	23.6%
1965	55–60	43	38	37	23	22.4
1970	50–55	47	38	36	22	22.6
1975	50–55	50	40	38	22	20.6

European data are from Statistical Office of the European Community, *Social Indicators for the European Community* (Luxembourg: 1977), table III/3, pp. 132–33. U.S. data are from U.S. Bureau of Labor Statistics, *Directory of National Unions and Employee Associations, 1977* (Washington, D.C.: U.S. Government Printing Office, 1979), p. 61.

Notes

On strikes the figures are:

Working Days Lost Annually through Industrial Disputes per 1000 Employees

Year	Italy	United States	France	United Kingdom	West Germany	Nether-lands
1960	486	377	82	138	2	140
1965	583	378	68	127	2	15
1970	1445	945	110	489	4	69
1975	1668	394	232	265	3	0
1976	1192	468	298	150	26	4

SOURCE: *Social Indicators,* table III/4, pp. 132–33. U.S. data calculated from U.S. Bureau of Labor Statistics, *Handbook of Labor Statistics 1978* (Washington, D.C.: Government Printing Office, 1979), p. 509.

For the greater part of the postwar era, Britain enjoyed comparative industrial peace:

Days Lost per 1,000 Persons Employed in Mining, Manufacturing, Construction, and Transport

Country	1955–64	1968–77
United States	1,044	1,340
Italy	875	1,914
West Germany	703	53
Canada	597	1,893
Japan	391	241
France	336	280
United Kingdom	294	850

SOURCE: Royal Commission on Trade Unions and Employers' Associations, *Written Evidence of the Ministry of Labor* (Her Majesty's Stationery Office, 1965), appendix XVI, p. 69. Reprinted in Lloyd Ulman, "Collective Bargaining and Industrial Efficiency," in Richard E. Caves, et al., *Britain's Economic Prospects* (Washington, D.C.: Brookings Institution, 1968), p. 333. The 1968–77 figures are from *The Economist*, 10 November 1979, p. 32.

5. See, for illustrations, Max Wilkinson "The Bizarre Troubles and Worries of Fleet Street," *Financial Times* (London), 18 May 1978; Paul Routledge, "A New Miners' Battle is Looming," *The Times* (London), 3 July 1978; or Ian Hargreaves and Christian Tyler, "Swan Hunter May Lose Another Deal," *Financial Times* (London), 27 January 1978. Shipbuilding, newspapers, and mining are notable cases, but not the only ones.

6. Speech by Lord Rothschild, head of the Central Policy Review Staff, to the Letcombe Laboratory of the Agricultural Research Council at Wantage,

Berkshire, 25 September 1973.

The Hudson Report on the United Kingdom, published for the Hudson Institute Europe by Associated Business Programmes, 21 November 1974.

7. This dispatch was dated 31 March 1979 and was published, virtually in full, in *The Economist,* 2 June 1979, pp. 29–40.

Recent efforts along the same line by other hands include Stephen Haseler, *The Death of British Democracy* (Buffalo, N.Y.: Prometheus Books, 1976); Robert Moss, *The Collapse of Democracy* (London: Sphere Books, 1975, 1977); Robert Emmett Tyrrell, Jr., ed., *The Future That Doesn't Work: Social Democracy's Failure in Britain* (Garden City, N.Y.: Doubleday, 1977).

8. Bernard Nossiter, *Britain: A Future That Works* (London: Deutsch, 1978).

9. As this is a matter of public controversy in Great Britain, the figures on economic centralization are calculated differently by those holding different political views. A strongly Tory position is argued by Eldon Griffiths, a Conservative M.P. for East Anglia, who in a letter to the *Telegraph* (24 June 1978) said:

> Getting on for 60 percent of all Britain's goods and services are now disposed of by government departments, local councils, the nationalized industries, and subsidies. Nearly one third of the wages and salaries earned by the British people, and close to two-thirds of the earnings of our private companies, are taken away from them in taxes and other state or local imposts.

By another calculation, the volume of public consumption as a percentage of gross domestic product, according to OECD figures in Great Britain, was second only to Sweden in Western Europe in 1975, at 19 percent, with the post office, telecommunications, electricity, gas, coal, railways, and shipbuilding all in the public sector, with airlines and steel mostly in the public sector, and with auto manufacture about half in the public sector. See *The Economist,* 4 March 1978, pp. 92–93.

10. White Paper on Employment Policy (London: Her Majesty's Stationery Office, 1944).

11. See Steven K. Bailey, *Congress Makes a Law* (New York: Columbia University Press, 1950).

12. The Beveridge Report on Social Security in 1943 was as significant as the White Paper on Employment Policy, and heralded the assumption by government of vastly extended powers in the social field as well (Sir William Beveridge, *Social Insurance and Allied Services,* CMND 6404, Parliamentary Session 1942–43, vol. 6, p. 119).

13. Peter Jay, *A General Hypothesis of Employment, Inflation and Politics,* the sixth Wincott memorial lecture (London: Institute of Economic Affairs, 1976).

14. See James Alt, *The Politics of Economic Decline* (Cambridge: Cambridge University Press, 1979).

15. A good review of trade union power is contained in "Schools Brief," *The*

Notes

Economist, 23 February 1980, pp. 68–69. A graph on p. 69 shows a sharp upturn in days lost to work stoppages in the 1970s as compared with the 1960s, with 1979 exhibiting far and away the worst postwar record.

16. Barbara Castle, *In Place of Strife,* an official white paper (CMND 3888), 1969.
17. Indeed, 1972 was by far the worst year for work stoppages in postwar Britain until 1979 broke the record.
18. Harold Macmillan, *At the End of the Day: 1961–63* (London: Macmillan, 1973), pp. 35–36.
19. Speech to the Conservative Party Conference at Blackpool, 14 October 1972; reported in *The Times* (London) on 16 October.

Chapter 2

1. First published in 1867, it is still in print (London: Collins, Fontana Library, 1963).
2. All of Great Britain appears to the outsider to operate on the "need to know" principle: if you have to ask, you probably are not supposed to have the information. None of the famous men's clubs of Pall Mall, for instance, have identifying signs on their imposing buildings. Indeed, why should they? Members know which is which, and it is nobody else's business. This sign frequently hangs on the public entrance to the Houses of Parliament, at St. Stephen's Gate: "Public Not Admitted." Members of the public who have business there are supposed to know that the message does not apply to them.
3. We do not pretend to exhaustiveness in our survey, but as a start can identify the Right Honorable Michael Stewart (born 1906), sometime Undersecretary of State for War, and later Foreign Secretary; Michael James Stewart (born 1933), sometime special adviser to the Secretary of State for Trade, and adviser to the Kenya Treasury and the Malta Labour party; and Sir Michael Stewart (born 1911), former minister of Her Majesty to Washington, ambassador to Greece, and genial host at Ditchley Park.
4. An exception that proves the rule is the case of the Conservative M.P. with the un-British name of William Van Straubenzee. His family, he says, has been British since 1745; and yet in 1978 he was able to fill a column of the *Guardian* with jocular complaints about the troubles that attend having an unfamiliar name in Great Britain. "A lady," he writes, "presiding over a luncheon at which I was advocating that Britain should remain in the Common Market during the referendum campaign ended her charming introduction with the words: 'And ladies, I have been sitting next to Mr. Van Straubenzee throughout lunch and he speaks English very nicely indeed!' " ("Grass Rooting," *The Guardian,* 15 May 1978).
5. See, for examples, Brian Lee, "Letter From Haltwhistle" (*Encounter,* February 1978, pp. 25–35), and John Weightman, "Haltwhistle Remembered" (*Encounter,* May 1978, pp. 41–44), for examinations of differences between

the dialects of East Northumbria and West Northumbria; or Roy Hatters-
ley's remarkable memoir *Goodbye to Yorkshire* (London: Victor Gollancz,
1976).

6. Technically "Ulster" refers to nine counties in the north of Ireland; politically
   and colloquially the term refers to the six of the nine incorporated into the
   current Northern Ireland.

7. A searing account of the famines of the 1840s, and of the misguided and
   callous English response, is Cecil Woodham-Smith's *The Great Hunger* (New
   York: Signet, 1964).

8. Douglas Hurd, *An End to Promises: Sketch of a Government, 1970–1974*
   (London: Collins, 1979).

9. An extensive study of the problem of Northern Ireland is Richard Rose,
   Governing without Consensus (Boston: Beacon, 1971).

10. The late John Mackintosh, Labour M.P. for Berwick and East Lothian,
    published a short but notable work on this theme in 1969: *The Devolution of
    Power* (London: Chatto and Windus, 1968).

11. Royal Commission on the Constitution, 1969–73, vol. I, *Report* (London:
    Her Majesty's Stationery Office, October 1973), CMND 5460.

12. Royal Commission on the Constitution, 1969–73, vol. II, *Memorandum of
    Dissent,* by Lord Crowther-Hunt and Professor A. T. Peacock (London: Her
    Majesty's Stationery Office, October 1973) CMND 5460–1.

13. See Iain McLean, "Devolution," *Political Quarterly* (April–June 1976) 47:
    221–27; and Jack Brand, *The National Movement in Scotland* (London:
    Routledge & Kegan Paul, 1978).

14. John L. L. Hammond, *Gladstone and the Irish Nation* (London, New York:
    Longmans Green, 1938).

15. Royal Commission *Report,* p. 247. Scotland is overrepresented at Westmin-
    ster compared with England. This is a deliberate policy because the country
    is more distant from Westminster and because large parts of it are thinly
    populated. If Scotland were to be equally represented, it would have only
    fifty-seven seats.

16. Among postwar elections, only in 1945 and 1966 did Labour have a comfort-
    able majority without taking account of Scottish seats.

17. Of the seventy-one Scottish seats in 1978, Labour held forty-one; the Conser-
    vatives, sixteen; the SNP, eleven; and Liberals, three.

18. The much-regretted premature death in August 1978 of John Mackintosh,
    a formidable speechmaker who would have led the Labour pro-devolution
    forces, also greatly crippled the government side in Scotland.

19. The New Commonwealth refers to those countries that received their inde-
    pendence and became full members from 1947 onward. That was the year in
    which India, Pakistan, and Ceylon (now Sri Lanka) became independent.
    Before that, only the old white dominions of Australia, New Zealand, Can-
    ada, and South Africa were full members apart from Britain. "New Com-
    monwealth" has therefore become a euphemism for the non-white members
    of the Commonwealth. In mid-1976, 1,776,000 persons were classified as

members of ethnic minority groups, or roughly 3.3 percent of the British population. The largest group were West Indians (604,000), followed by Indians (390,000), Pakistani and Bangladeshi (246,000), African Asians (160,000), Cypriots and Maltese (159,000), Far Easterners (115,000) from Hong Kong, Singapore, Malaysia, Samoa, and so on, and Africans (97,000). These statistics, from official sources, were published in Joe Rogaly, "Mrs. Thatcher and the Facts," *Financial Times* (London), 1 February 1978. We have found Mr. Rogaly's work on this issue of great value.

20. A treatment sympathetic to Mrs. Thatcher can be read in Peter Gill, "Mrs. Thatcher Tries to Calm Immigrant Fears," *Telegraph* (London), 15 July 1978. See also Rogaly, "Mrs. Thatcher and the Facts."

21. Here, for example, is Richard Crossman's view from the left wing of the Labour party in 1965: ". . . we have to combine tight immigration controls, even if it means changing the law, with a constructive policy for integrating into the community the immigrants who are there already. This has been my line as a Midland MP and here I really do represent my constituents. Ever since the Smethwick election it has been quite clear that immigration can be the greatest potential vote-loser for the Labour Party if we are seen to be permitting a flood of immigrants to come in and blight the central areas in all our cities" (*The Diaries of a Cabinet Minister,* vol. I [New York: Holt, Rinehart & Winston, 1975], pp. 149–50).

Chapter 3

1. See Nicholas Mansergh, *The Commonwealth Experience* (London: Weidenfeld & Nicholson, 1969).

2. Two important works on Suez are Leon D. Epstein, *British Politics in the Suez Crisis* (Urbana: University of Illinois Press, 1964); and Selwyn Lloyd, *Suez 1956: A Personal Account* (London: Jonathan Cape, 1978). See also Michael Howard, "Suez: The Fatal Operation," *The Sunday Times,* 9 July 1978; Hugh Thomas, *The Suez Affair* (London: Weidenfeld, 1966); and Richard E. Neustadt, *Alliance Politics* (New York: Columbia University Press, 1970).

3. See Seymour Martin Lipset, "The Polls on the Middle East," *Middle East Review,* Fall 1978, pp. 24–30.

4. The effects of North Sea oil on British needs has been dramatic. Here are the figures:

Degree of Dependence on Foreign Oil Supply
(Net imports of energy as a percentage of Gross Inland Consumption and Storage)

Year	United Kingdom	United States
1970	50.3	12.1

Year	United Kingdom	United States
1971	*54.8*	——
1972	*54.8*	*15.5*
1973	*53.1*	*19.2*
1974	*55.7*	*19.3*
1975	*48.3*	*19.3*
1976	*43.9*	*22.1*
1977	*30.3*	*25.6*
1978	*25.7*	*23.6*

SOURCE: Statistical Office of the European Commission, *Basic Statistics of the Community* (Luxembourg: 1979), table 52, pp. 74–75; and U.S. Bureau of the Census, *Statistical Abstract of the United States* (Washington D.C.: Government Printing Office, 1979), p. 601.

5. Britain, Norway, Denmark, Sweden, Austria, Switzerland, and Portugal.

6. See Robert J. Lieber's excellent overview, *British Politics and European Unity* (Berkeley: University of California Press, 1970).

7. A verbatim rendering of General de Gaulle's remarks appears in "Excerpts from Remarks by de Gaulle," *New York Times,* 15 January 1963, p. 2.

8. For an account of this disastrous meeting and its context, see Neustadt, *Alliance Politics.*

9. Acheson speech at West Point, reported the next day in the *New York Times* (6 December 1962).

10. See Ian S. McDonald, ed., *Anglo-American Relations since the Second World War* (New York: St. Martin's, 1974), pp. 101ff.; and H. G. Nicholas, *The United States and Britain* (Chicago: University of Chicago Press, 1975).

11. 24 March 1979.

12. See Edward F. Denison, "Economic Growth," in Richard E. Caves, ed., *Britain's Economic Prospects* (Washington: Brookings, 1968), pp. 254–57.

13. *The Sunday Times* (London), 1 June 1980..

14. U.S. Bureau of the Census, *Statistical Abstract of the United States* (Washington, D.C.: Government Printing Office, 1979), p. 33, shows U.S. population by ethnic origin as of 1973 and, on pp. 886–87, gives 1971 figures for the United Kingdom and for Ireland.

	In United States	In United Kingdom
English	25,993,000	55,515,000
Irish	12,240,000	In Ireland 2,978,000

See also William Shannon, *The American Irish* (New York: Macmillan, 1963).

15. Report of the Committee on Representational Services Overseas appointed by the Prime Minister under the Chairmanship of Lord Plowden (CMND 2276), 1962–63 2 December 1963).
16. Report of the Review Committee on Overseas Representation; chairman, Sir Val Duncan (CMND 4107), 1968–69 (1969).
17. *Review of Overseas Representation.* Report by the Central Policy Review Staff (London: Her Majesty's Stationery Office, 1977).
18. Indeed, it was disastrously received. See *The Times* (London) leader, "A Report with Few Friends," 14 April 1978; "MPs Find 'Confusion over Nature of Power,' " *Financial Times* (London), 14 April 1978; Richard Norton-Taylor, "Think Tank 'Folly' Attacked by MPs" and "MPs Back the Role of Britain's Diplomats," *The Guardian* (Manchester and London), 14 April 1978; "Old Possum's Book of Practical Cuts," editorial, *The Guardian,* 14 April 1978; an entire page in the *Daily Telegraph* (London) headed "All-Party Committee of MPs Flays 'Think Tank' Proposals," 14 April 1978; and Max Beloff, "The Think Tank and Foreign Affairs," *Public Administration* (Winter 1977) 55:435–44.

Chapter 4

1. There is some evidence that the personality of the individual candidate is coming to matter more in British politics, but the broad generalization is still justified. See Bruce E. Cain, John A. Ferejohn, and Morris P. Fiorina, "The House Is Not a Home: MPs and Their Constituencies," prepared for Midwest Political Science Association Meeting, 29 April 1979.
2. One indication of the centrality of party competition in British political culture is the famous argument that it is necessary for the House of Commons to be shaped so that government and opposition sit facing one another in confrontation, rather than in the allegedly less adversarial fan shape facing toward a common rostrum as is typical in legislatures not based on the Westminster model. See S. E. Finer, *Adversary Politics and Electoral Reform* (London: Anthony Wigram, 1975).
3. See Douglas Schoen, *Enoch Powell and the Powellites* (London: Macmillan, 1977); David Coates, *The Labour Party and the Struggle for Socialism* (Cambridge: Cambridge University Press, 1975); and D. Howell, *British Social Democracy* (London: Croom Helm, 1976).
4. The term was coined by *The Economist* and combines the names of two successive chancellors of the Exchequer—the Labourite Hugh Gaitskell and the Conservative R. A. Butler (now Lord Butler).
5. See the splendid biography by Bernard Donoughue and G. W. Jones, *Herbert Morrison: Portrait of a Politician* (London: Weidenfeld & Nicolson, 1973).
6. See David Butler and Donald Stokes, *Political Change in Britain* (New York: St. Martin, 1974), for an elaborate discussion of political attitudes of British voters.
7. Two good sources on the prime ministry of Harold Wilson are Joe Haines, *The Politics of Power* (Sevenoaks, Kent: Hodder & Stoughton, 1977); and

Marcia Williams, *Inside Number 10* (New York: Coward, McCann, 1972).

8. A definitive biography of Gaitskell is Phillip Williams, *Hugh Gaitskell: A Political Biography* (London: Jonathan Cape, 1979).

9. See Howard Penniman, ed. *Britain at the Polls* (Washington: American Enterprise Institute, 1975).

10. See Peter Jenkins, *The Battle of Downing Street* (London: Knight, 1970).

11. Anthony Crosland, *The Future of Socialism* (London: Jonathan Cape, 1956).

12. Crosland, in Dick Leonard, ed. *Socialism Now and Other Essays* (London: Jonathan Cape, 1974), p. 26.

13. See Richard Rose, *Politics in England* (Boston: Little, Brown, 1974), p. 290: "A comparative study of postwar voting trends in nineteen western nations found Britain the most static system, because of the lack of long-term change in party support since 1945, and because of the low fluctuations in party votes between elections." Butler and Stokes, *Political Change in Britain,* argue that while the ideas of "left" and "right" may exist in élite political discourse, they have little meaning to ordinary voters. We adopt the conventional terminology here so as to describe the inferences about appropriate partisan behavior that politicians commonly make in conceptualizing their world in this fashion.

14. All 635 members of the House of Commons are elected in general elections for five years or until Parliament is dissolved. Between general elections, when a seat falls vacant owing to the resignation or the death of a member, a by-election is held. The results of these overall tend to go against the party controlling the government.

15. Speech to the Conservative Party Conference at Blackpool on 7 October 1975; reported in *The Times* (London) on 8 October.

16. Modern Conservative free marketers have assumed only part of the Gladstonian heritage: economic liberalism but not the emphasis upon social improvement. See Ian Bradley, "Liberalism: A Victorian Legacy," *The Listener,* 28 June 1979.

17. Figures in *Public Opinion* (June–July, 1979, p. 54) show an eleven-point shift toward the Tories among skilled workers from October 1974 to May 1979. Unskilled workers, far more pro-Labour in their sentiments, moved 6.5 percent toward the Tories; and the lower-middle class became 4.5 percent more Conservative over the same period. Conservatives gained more among men than among women (9.5 percent versus 3 percent) and in all age groups, but gained most among youngest voters (a gain of 9.5 percent in the 18–24 age bracket) and less as voters grew older. The figures comport with the general tendency repeatedly observed in many settings for party loyalty to stabilize with age.

18. The terms of the pact were that the Liberals undertook to sustain the Labour government in office but not to support every item of government policy. This meant that they were bound to vote with the government on any vote of confidence, but were free to vote against it on anything that was not made a matter of confidence. They did indeed help to secure the government's

defeat on a number of questions, including important provisions of the Finance Bill shortly after the pact was formed. In return for keeping the government in office, an elaborate process was established for regular consultation between Labour ministers and Liberal parliamentary spokesmen in their respective fields. See Alistair Michie and Simon Hoggart, *The Pact* (London: Quartet, 1978).

19. This analysis seems to be consistent with the argument in W. L. Miller's "Social Class and Party Choice in England," *British Journal of Political Science* (July 1978) 8: 257–84. See also the analysis in Peter Kellner, "Election Season: Labour's Shifting Support," *New Statesman,* 23 June 1978, pp. 838–40; "What Future for Britain's Two-Party System?" *The Economist,* 11 March 1978, pp. 22–25; and Ivor Crewe, Bo Särlvik and James Alt, "Partisan Dealignment in Britain 1964–74," *British Journal of Political Science* (April 1977) 7: 129–90.

20 See, for example Evan Luard, *Socialism without the State* (London: Macmillan, 1979); and David Marquand, "Taming Leviathan: Social Democracy and Decentralization," *Socialist Commentary* (February 1980).

Chapter 5

1. Membership in the European Community has brought an important modification to the principle of parliamentary sovereignty. EEC laws and regulations made in Brussels automatically have effect in the United Kingdom, as in all other member countries. The British Parliament can neither veto nor amend them. It tries to exercise its influence by considering proposals for Community legislation before they are passed. Both the House of Commons and the House of Lords have set up a committee for this purpose. The respective committees operate on slightly different lines. The House of Commons committee draws the attention of the House to any proposal that it regards as particularly important or contentious. This arrangement does not work well, partly because there is not sufficient parliamentary time to give proper consideration to all the matters referred by the committee, partly because many proposals are produced by the commission at the last minute for consideration by the Council of Ministers, and partly because proposals are often amended considerably in the course of council debates. Even though each member government is represented on the council, it is impossible for a national legislature to have a direct effect on the outcome unless it is prepared to tie the hands of its minister. Only the Danish parliament, the *Folketing,* has a committee that can go that far. The volume and the range of Community legislation will increase over the years. At the moment it provides an important exception to the doctrine of parliamentary sovereignty but does not destroy it.

2. See Leon D. Epstein, *Political Parties in Western Democracies* (London: Pall Mall Press, 1967), pp. 315–18, for a compact discussion of the logic of party discipline in parliamentary systems.

3. Neville Chamberlain resigned as Prime Minister in 1940 because he was deserted on a critical vote by many of his own backbenchers. This, however, was not a case of the government's being defeated on a vote of confidence; it was a psychological blow that so undermined his personal authority as Prime Minister that he felt it to be inappropriate, and possibly even impossible, to go on. In 1931 the Labour government of the day split over whether to make severe cuts in public expenditure in the attempt to keep Britain on the gold standard. Before that, one can go back beyond Ramsay Mac-Donald's 1924 defeat to 1922 and the fall of Lloyd George's coalition government after the First World War. That government fell because it was decided at a meeting of the Conservative party in the Carlton Club that the Conservatives, who had a majority of members in the House of Commons, should withdraw support from the coalition.

4. As we shall shortly see, the operations of this convention have not precluded considerable restiveness on the part of backbenchers, especially in recent years. The time may be approaching when those scholars who point to the increase in this phenomenon will gain general assent to the notion that this convention is eroding. See Philip Norton, "The Changing Face of the House of Commons in the 1970's," *Legislative Studies Quarterly* (August 1980); John E. Schwarz, "Exploring a New Role in Policy Making: The British House of Commons in the 1970's," *American Political Science Review* (March 1980) 74: 23–37; John E. Schwarz, "The Commons Bites Back," *Financial Times* (London), 2 June 1978.

5. See Geoffrey Smith, "The Heyday of the Party Rebel," *The Times* (London), 12 May 1978.

6. Parliamentary correspondent Andrew Roth has made an effort to keep track of the outside activities of M.P.'s. See Roth, *The Business Background of MP's* (London: Parliamentary Profiles, 1975). On the level of compensation, a comparison as of 1975 between M.P.'s and members of Congress can be found in Nelson W. Polsby, "Legislatures," in Fred I. Greenstein and Nelson W. Polsby, *Handbook of Political Science,* vol. 5 (Reading, Mass.: Addison-Wesley, 1975), p.306. When the European Parliament was set up, the issue of compensation for members arose, and policy makers had to confront the vastly differing pay scales for legislators in Western democracies. *The Economist* (9 December 1978, p. 19) printed the following table, with Britain far toward the bottom:

189

Notes

National MPs Pre-Tax Pay (1977)*	Pounds per annum
Germany	22,700
Belgium	21,500
France	21,000
Holland	19,530
Denmark	11,750
Italy	10,500
Ireland	6,273
Britain	6,270
Luxembourg	4,500

*Excluding allowances, which vary greatly.

7. On the work load of the individual member, see Frances Morrell *From the Electors of Bristol* (London: Spokesman Pamphlet 57, 1977); Bruce George, "Grassrooting," *The Guardian* 8 May 1978; Joy Tagner, "Worth Her Wage in Votes," *Observer Review,* 26 February 1978; and various unpublished papers by Bruce Cain and his colleagues at California Institute of Technology.

8. One transatlantic look is Geoffrey Smith, *Westminster Reform: Learning From Congress* (London: Trade Policy Research Centre, Thames Essays, 1979).

9. A general treatment comparing legislatures in a variety of systems is Polsby, "Legislatures."

10. This sentiment was expressed in much of the commentary on the occasion of the report of the Select Committee on Procedure (House of Commons Paper 588–8; London: Her Majesty's Stationery Office, 1978) that led to the strengthening of parliamentary committees. See, for example, David Wood, "When House Theatre Gives Way to Reason," *The Times* (London) 3 April 1978; "Waiting for a Report on Select Committees," *The Times* (London) 4 April 1978. This last is a verbatim report of colloquy in the House.

11. These are known, according to British practice, as "select committees," but it was recommended that they operate roughly as weakened versions of what in U.S. congressional jargon would be known as "standing committees."

12. Select Committee report.

13. These were the general subcommittee, which examined economic policy as a whole; defense and external affairs; trade and industry; education and the arts; environment and the Home Office; and employment and social services.

14. See Geoffrey Smith, *Westminster Reform: Learning from Congress,* where these ideas are developed at greater length. After a consolidated fund bill had received its second reading, giving approval in principle, on the floor of the House, it would then be sent to the select committees for its committee stage, where each clause would be examined and possibly amended. The bill would be divided so that each committee would examine the proposed expenditure

190

for the particular government department it was covering. The Treasury select committee would look at the bill as a whole. This committee would be able to change the distribution of funds among departments and to reduce the total estimates, but not to raise them. Other committees would be able to change the distribution of funds among different functions on a departmental vote and to reduce that vote, but not to raise it. There would then be no danger of this procedure leading to competing claims for higher public expenditure. The bill as amended would then come back to the floor of the House for its report stage—as is the practice with all other bills—so that no committee would have the final word.

15. See John Whale, "At War with Whitehall," *Sunday Times* (London), 22 January 1978; and Rupert Cornwell, "Senior MPs Will Discuss Sackings" *Financial Times* (London), 13 March 1978. The abrupt change of committee members—to an American observer a remarkable event—made only the smallest ripple in the British press.

16. Quinton McGarel Hogg, Baron Hailsham of St. Marylebone, *The Dilemma of Democracy: Diagnosis and Prescription* (London: Collins, 1978).

17. The latest occasion on which the Supreme Court has seen fit to pronounce on the qualifications of Congressmen is *Powell* v. *McCormack* 395 U.S. 486 (1969).

18. For an elaborated discussion of the differences between legislative arenas and more transformative legislatures, see Polsby, "Legislatures."

Chapter 6

1. The one exception to this second rule is that some principal ambassadorships are occasionally held by outsiders. Peter Jay, who was ambassador in Washington from 1977 to 1979, went direct to that office from journalism, and left diplomacy as soon as he ceased to be ambassador. Similarly, Lord Soames, the Conservative cabinet minister, was for some years ambassador in Paris. But these instances do not affect the general pattern.

2. Not since 1954—when Sir Thomas Dugdale insisted on resigning as minister of agriculture over an issue concerning the return to private hands of a piece of land requisitioned by the government during the Second World War, in which a civil servant was in error though without any suspicion of corruption —has a minister left any government on the grounds of dereliction of ministerial responsibility. This was the Crichel Down case.

3. Minority introduction written by Brian Sedgemore to the Eleventh Report from the Expenditure Committee for Session 1976–77: *The Civil Service* (London: Her Majesty's Stationery Office, 1977). Mr. Sedgemore was a left-wing Labour M.P. who subsequently lost his seat. The proposal to include his chapter as part of the full report was lost in the committee by 15 votes to 11.

Notes

4. Richard Crossman, *The Diaries of a Cabinet Minister,* 3 vols. (London: Hamilton, 1975–77). See the sharply critical review of the third volume by George Jones, in *Socialist Commentary* (December 1977). The tensions between ministers and civil servants are the source of a successful BBC television comedy series by Antony Jay and Jonathan Lynn, "Yes, Minister."

5. "Westminster and Whitehall: Adapting to Change," lecture by William Rodgers, M.P., to the Royal Institute of Public Administration on 5 November 1979.

6. Granada television program, *World in Action*—"Mr. Benn's Secret Service," 7 January 1980.

7. These are specific instances, though we must add in fairness that Mr. Benn is a controversial witness, and that the Civil Service interpretation has not been heard.

8. In May 1980 the Prime Minister appointed an independent inquiry to consider the method of valuation of index-linked pensions in the public sector. The advantage of having such a pension is supposed to be taken into account in pay settlements, but there has been a widespread feeling for some time that, in an age of inflation, the deductions from pay made on account of such pensions do not represent their full value to the recipients.

9. Rodgers, "Westminster and Whitehall."

10. *Eleventh Report from the Expenditure Committee,* "The Civil Service," vol. 1, pp. 535–I (London: Her Majesty's Stationery Office, July 1977).

11. The leading critic of the Civil Service on grounds of biased recruitment is Lord Crowther-Hunt who, in the words of the report "accepts that 'if the civil service is seeking to recruit the most able people it is hardly surprising that Oxbridge supplies a higher proportion than other universities' " (*Eleventh Report,* p.xix).

12. Ibid., p.xx.

13. Rodgers, "Westminster and Whitehall."

14. *The Civil Service,* vol. 1. Report of the Committee 1966–68, Chairman: Lord Fulton, CMND 3638 (June 1968).

15. At the request of the Ministry of Aviation, an official inquiry was conducted by Sir John Lang, a former Civil Service head of the Admiralty, and two others. Their principal report was published in July 1964: *First Report of the Inquiry into the Pricing of Ministry of Aviation Contracts* (London: Her Majesty's Stationery Office, 1964).

16. Report by the Committee of Inquiry appointed by the Minister of Overseas Development into the circumstances that led to the Crown agents requesting financial assistance from the government in 1974 (London: Her Majesty's Stationery Office, 1977).

17. Granada Television program, *World in Action*—"Mr. Benn's Secret Service," 7 January 1980.

18. Among the new select committees, the Treasury and Civil Service Select Committee has appointed advisers of exceptionally high quality from the

London Business School, the Cambridge Department of Applied Economics, and a leading stockbroker, Philips and Drew.

19. See "Letter to a Special Adviser," *The Economist,* 26 May 1979, p.24; and Rudolf Klein and Janet Lewis, "Advice and Dissent in British Government: The Case of the Special Advisers," *Policy and Politics* (September 1977) 6:1–25).

20. *The Economist* 18 November 1978, p. 109) published a short list of distinguished defecters from the senior Civil Service to private employment.

Chapter 7

1. The figures are startling in two ways: first, the gap between the United States and the United Kingdom; and, second, the deplorable increases visible in both countries during the 1970s.

Homicides per 100,000 Residents

	1950	1955	1960	1965	1970	1975
United States	5.2%	4.5	4.7	5.5	8.3	10.0
(actual number)	(7,942)	(7,418)	(8,464)	(10,712)	(16,848)	(21,310)
United Kingdom	0.77%*	0.7	0.6	0.7	3.1	3.3†
(actual number)	(313)	(297)	(289)	(317)	(1,487)	(1,611)

*UK figures for 1951.
†UK figures for 1973.

SOURCES: For the United States, Bureau of The Census, *Statistical Abstract of the U.S.* (Washington, D.C.: Government Printing Office, 1979), p. 33. For the United Kingdom, Statistical Office, *Demographic Yearbook* (New York: United Nations, 1953, 1961, 1975), pp. 256 (1953), 463–64 (1961), and 766–67, 827–28 (1975).

We wonder if the flowering of the literary genre of the murder mystery in Great Britain is related to the rarity of homicide. In a culture where murder is an unusual and hence shocking event, it needs to be explained on a case-by-case basis—if possible, by an eccentric detective.

2. See "Motorway Madness," *The Economist,* 7 July 1979, p. 124.

3. See Mark DeWolfe Howe, *The Holmes-Laski Letters,* vol. I (Cambridge, Mass.: Harvard University Press, 1953), p. 421.

4. There is some evidence of a brain drain in the business sector. A survey

reported in *Business Week* (23 May 1977, p. 46) indicates that, in 1976, 27 percent of the top managers in 375 large British corporations pursued opportunities overseas—up from 14 percent in 1975; and that, between 1974 and 1977, "more than 100,000 executives, middle-managers and entrepreneurs are believed to have quit Britain."

5. An excellent portrait of the ideology of that period is Ralph Waldo Emerson's *English Traits* (Boston: Houghton Mifflin, 1876). For a more modern account, see James Morris, *Pax Britannica: The Climax of an Empire* (New York: Harcourt Brace, 1968), and *Heaven's Command: An Imperial Progress* (New York: Harcourt Brace, 1974).

INDEX

195

Index

196

Index

Index

Index